Dying to
Go on Vacation

Marty J. Cauley

LIVE PASSIONATELY!

Hebrews 12

ISBN-13: 978-0692491140 (Marbles Press)

ISBN-10: 0692491147

Dedication

To the two women in my life that held me together before, during, and after my first twenty-eight days dying. My wife, Danelle, who daily walks with me through the valley of the shadow of death and the forest of ambiguity. My daughter, Lydia, whose sunny disposition and determination inspire me to keep fighting. I love you!

To Garry & Virginia who have been with Danelle and me from the first day to the worst days. Now you are facing your journey with cancer, we are with you all the way!

Contents

Introduction: My First Twenty-Eight Days Dying

"We must accept finite disappointment, but we must never lose infinite hope."
Martin Luther King, Jr., pastor & civil rights leader

I know the plans I have in mind for you, declares the Lord; they are plans for peace, not disaster, to give you a future filled with hope. Jeremiah 29:11

Do not wait until you are dying to go on vacation. I think if I had to give you one piece of advice that would be it. We put things off. We do not mean to, but we do. We carry around the assumption that there is plenty of time to do whatever needs to be done. We say we understand life is fleeting, but we act as though it is endless. Then something happens and reminds us that it is not.

This is a story that begins and ends "on vacation." Never in my life have I had two "vacations" within twenty-eight days. For a workaholic like me, that is absurd. For somebody who has derived most of his self worth from vocational and academic achievement, taking vacations was a luxury I thought I could ill afford. The vacation at the beginning of this journey was the first vacation of more than four days that my wife and I have taken in seven years. Never in our life together had we afforded ourselves the chance to get away for so long. It was during this vacation that I learned that I had cancer. The vacation at the end of this journey was taken to help me recover physically from being in the hospital and mentally/emotionally from learning that my life will end far sooner than I ever imagined. Through the generosity of an anonymous donor, my family was given a week at a beach house at the Outer Banks of North Carolina. During this second vacation, I began recording my ideas about this experience. Life is full of ironies. One irony is that it took this kind of devastating experience to get my attention and to take a vacation (two!) with my family.

I am dying. That's the prognosis. In typical medical lingo the doctors have been overwhelmingly vague about how quickly I am dying, but they pretty much agree that barring something miraculous, I am dying. When we finally asked the oncologist point blank how much time I had left, she answered that I might live for many months. She did not say years at the first visit. She ordered some additional tests and told us that she needed to track the growth rate of the tumors over time to see how quickly they are growing. My wife, Danelle, told me much of the conversation later because my brain had stopped processing after hearing "many months." Many months. I might make it to Christmas. How many months *is* many?

There is really nothing you can do to get ready to hear that you are dying except to live every day with passion and intensity, so that when the day comes that somebody puts a fairly small number on the days you have left, you will have no regrets for not having lived. Even after you hear it you kind of stagger backwards (metaphorically speaking, because hopefully you are sitting down when you hear that kind of news) and try to make sure what you thought you heard, you actually heard. Your head starts spinning. Your world starts shifting. You now have the unbelievable realization of the finite nature of your existence. Your head swims as you try to figure out how to get ready for what you now know is coming really soon that you had hoped to put off for a few decades. I mean come on; at 48 years old I am just now in "middle age." That would seem to imply that I should live at least 48 more years?

Suddenly I began to realize that my middle age was when I was 25 or 26 because it looks like I will be meeting the Grim Reaper at around 50, and that sucks.

I do not have many regrets. Oh, I have a few, but I am pretty sure everyone has a few. Mostly I have thanksgivings! I have experiences I am glad I had, like going to Africa and meeting the orphans my congregation has sponsored for the past couple of years. I've done things like spending five years investing in youth and young adults in retreat ministry; that is one of the hallmarks of my career. I've preached a couple of thousand sermons where I have tried my best to explain to everyone who would listen that God loves them, Jesus died for them, and there is a divine calling for their lives. I am not sure many people listened. I know I have gotten through to a few, and for those I am eternally thankful.

Twenty-eight days ago I was in a hospital when I was told that I have cancer. For the record, that is pretty much the worst day of my life so far. I am hoping it stays at the top of the list because I'd hate to see what could top it. I guess if I also come down with leprosy, that would be pretty bad, but otherwise I am pretty sure that July 10, 2013 is going to top the list of my all-time bad days.

So for twenty-eight days I've been keenly aware that I am dying. It has been a tough twenty-eight days that has involved interminable amounts of waiting and not knowing what's next. It has involved more tears than I can ever remember crying. It has involved making lists. Lists of what I want to do before I die — like go back to Walt Disney World. Lists of things I'll never get to do— like see the diverse children my daughter plans to adopt. Lists of things I am really going to miss — like kissing my wife, cheeseburgers, and sunsets. And lists of things I am not going to miss at all — like taxes and manipulative church people.

For twenty-eight days I've watched my wife suffer knowing her husband is going to die. I have wanted to protect her from the pain that she is bearing; I have been completely unable to deliver her from it. It hangs on her soul like a weight that I would give anything to lift. For twenty-eight days, the love of my life has shouldered this burden that I cannot carry for her.

I have spent time memorizing every freckle on her back and every curl in her hair (that's a lot of memorizing). Thanks to the cancer, for the first time in my life I have insomnia, but that's okay because I have time to watch her sleep.

To make this time bearable for both of us we have talked, and talked a lot. We have discussed what we want to do, and what we do not want to waste time doing. We have talked about family relationships, money, mortgage, and when would be the right time for me to quit working full time. We have wept bitterly and laughed more than I ever thought I would. When you choose to live, you really begin to value the relationships that matter.

There is no manual on how to process bad news. There are strategies and suggestions, but everybody handles this kind of thing differently. The way Danelle and I have handled it is by being open and vulnerable with our fears, concerns, and hopes. We have also prayed about every aspect of the disease process and every decision we are making. Sometimes we pray just for the strength to make it through another day. While this has been our biggest trial, it has also been our greatest relational victory. It seems like we are literally traveling through, "the valley of the shadow of death," but we know we are not alone. We have each other and we know, ultimately, God is in control. It is amazing how much it means sometimes just to sit quietly on the sofa and hold the hand of the person who is traveling with you through a dark time in your life. Those times give me the ability to make it through and to keep going.

When you find out you are dying, it is easy to simply just quit living. If you have somebody who is committed, absolutely committed, to traveling with you, it gives you the ability to keep living, even when you are dying. Just like road trips are better with somebody you love riding shotgun, life is better when it's travelled with those who love you.

On Monday I went to see my oncologist for our second visit. I had several tests between visits and we were anxiously awaiting this appointment to review the results. I have since learned that the state of worry related to cancer tests is sarcastically called "scanxiety" by a lot of patients. The doctor went over the scans with us and showed me all the places where the neuroendocrine tumors (NETs) were attacking my body from the inside. It would be almost fascinating if it was not so devastating. My current prognosis is still serious but with treatment, care, and management I might yet have a few years to do productive work before the cancer spreads and the pain makes it difficult to think. We went from "many months" to "maybe a few years."

Now I look to the next twenty-eight days, and the twenty-eight days after that. I will turn to measuring my life in days and months rather than years and decades. So, as you read about these twenty-eight days, I want you to begin thinking and praying about your next twenty-eight days, and all the days after that, so that you won't wait until you are dying to plan your vacation. So that you do not quit living, just because you realize that you are dying.

Gracious God, help me to make the most of every day that You give me. Help me to seize the opportunities that You give me to love deeply, live passionately, and listen to You intentionally. In the name of the One who holds my tomorrow, Jesus, I pray. Amen.

Chapter 1 My Summer Vacation

*"I do not believe that sheer suffering teaches.
If sufferings alone taught, all the world would be wise, since everyone suffers.
To suffering must be added mourning, understanding, patience,
love, openness and willingness to remain vulnerable."*
Anne Morrow Lindbergh, pilot, poet, & writer

"Lord, you listen to the desires of those who suffer. You steady their hearts; you listen closely to them…" Psalm 10:17

When I was a kid it seemed that every school year began with having to write a story about your summer vacation. Stories of summer camp, beach trips, amusement parks, and lots of free time filled the morning as we all shared what happened to us during those precious, sun-filled months of summer. It's funny how I never remember anybody coming back from vacation saying that their entire life had been thrown on an emotional, spiritual, and physical roller coaster and they weren't sure when it would end. But that, my friends, is what happened during my "summer vacation."

This year my summer vacation began in a very uneventful way. For the first time in years Danelle and I had planned to get away for twelve days, in a row, together. On Wednesday morning we pulled out of the driveway and headed to Berkeley Springs, West Virginia. Berkeley Springs has a lot of unrealized potential as a romantic getaway spot. It has rolling mountain views, mineral springs bubbling through the town, spas, restaurants, and quaint little bed and breakfast places. It's cute, and I am sure some people really love it; we found it just "okay." Our B&B was nice, but the bed was lumpy and there was so much stuff in every room I was sure I was going to destroy something. The restaurants tried too hard and the food was just blah. The spa was nice but my massage therapist at home is far better, but no matter, it was two days of doing absolutely nothing, which was a time of Sabbath.

Friday we picked up our fourteen year old son, Jacob, from his grandparents and headed for Erie, Pennsylvania, which is Danelle's hometown. That evening we gathered with Danelle's two sisters and their respective spouses, children, and others and headed to Waldameer Amusement Park. It was a great evening riding classic rides and hanging out. Danelle and I even rode the Ravine Flyer II (though nobody could tell me what happened to Ravine Flyer I and that's disconcerting…LOL). This roller coaster is one of the top ten wooden coasters in the US. It creaks and pops and throws you around like you are in a washing machine. One curve was so hard I am sure I bruised a rib.

The next day the family gathered again for a pool party and cookout at a friend's home. There were lots of awesome "bad" foods (cheeseburgers, treats, etc.) and, beverages; as well as plenty of sunshine, and chlorinated water. After spending eighteen months on *Naturally Slim* I abandoned all positive dietary practices and ate way too much. That night I chewed TUMS and tried to recover from hours of over-indulgence.

Sunday morning dawned and we headed to worship at Christ United Methodist Church in Erie, PA. The people were friendly and the service was good, but I was having difficulty sitting still. I was anxious and my abdomen hurt. It was not like a typical stomachache, but constant with moments of stabbing pain. I have no idea what the pastor said (though Danelle said it was really good). When we arrived back at the room, we determined that I would skip the afternoon outing to the beach and try to get over this stomach thing so I could enjoy the dinner party that evening. At 9 am the pain was annoying; at noon it was disturbing and I couldn't get comfortable; at 3 pm the pain was becoming unbearable. I texted Danelle and told her to come get me; we needed to go to the hospital. I assumed that I was having a gall bladder attack in response to eating like an idiot the day before. I had already revisited the contents of my breakfast and some of the previous day's food so there was nothing left inside except for the pain.

After the longest ten-minute drive of my life, we arrived at St. Vincent Medical Center. The emergency room was packed with kids with ear infections, a soccer injury, a man who smelled of cheap alcohol, and the other colorful characters that populate the waiting area of any emergency room on a typical Sunday afternoon. We checked in and I proceeded to pace, or sit, or stand in the corner, completely unable to get comfortable. I have no idea how long we waited though it seemed like an eternity. We finally went back, and after a preliminary assessment the doctor ordered an IV with some pain meds (thanks be to God) and an ultrasound to confirm gall bladder involvement.

From this point on everything was filtered through a medically induced fog, which was mostly filled in later by Danelle who, all this time dressed in a bathing suit and cover dress, refused to leave my side.

We had the ultrasound, but as the tech was working something caught her eye. She took a picture, made notes, moved a centimeter, took more pictures, made notes. She hurried from the room to share the results with the attending physician. We headed back to the emergency room, but by the time we got there another transporter was there to take us for a CT scan, just to "confirm a few things" (great lesson here, medical people are the masters at being intentionally vague).

We had another scan, and then were eventually transported to a room on the eighth floor. Danelle went back to the hotel room to change and returned to spend the night on one of those super-comfy vinyl hospital recliners. You know the kind, the ones that squeak every time you move and have the vague aroma of hospital cleaner. The rest of the night is a blur of shots, vitals, meds, discomfort, and prayers. The staff on the eighth floor of the St. Vincent Medical Center is amazing. From the housekeeper to the unit secretary, every nurse, aide, and personal care assistant (PCA) were doing all they could to relieve the pain and help us get answers. This team was something special.

The next two days were pretty much a haze. There were more tests, lots of lab work, and more tests. The final test on Monday was a liver biopsy assisted by a CT scan. Sounds fun, huh? They essentially take a three-foot needle and stick it through your gut. Well, not all the way through, and it's probably not really three feet long, it just feels like it. After that test all other tests came to a screeching halt. In hindsight it was clear that the medical team had found out something conclusive and, therefore, did not need any further information. There is a time between the acquisition of the knowledge and the explanation of the findings that seems like an eternity. We entered that kind of medical twilight zone where the next couple of days were essentially relegated to waiting, worrying, and praying. Whatever it was, it was not going to be good, the sideways glances of the nursing staff betrayed the seriousness of the illness.

After two days being NPO (without food or water and only fed by IV fluids) I was allowed clear liquids, then a "soft diet" including the worst bagel of my life with some horrible eggs. Yep, hospital food is hospital food everywhere. I was moved to oral pain meds, IV fluids were slowed down, and my head began to clear. Danelle had spent hours and hours watching over me in our small room. We began to walk the halls, make lists, and do anything we could to occupy the time.

There were some early signs that things were far more serious than we had imagined when we arrived at the hospital. We had an initial consult with the admitting physician. He was a very straightforward young man and he let us know up front that they were testing for some form of pancreatic or hepatic cancer. He informed us that while it could be benign, he suspected that my condition was far more serious than previously considered.

While this was hard news, receiving it on Monday morning had given us some time to prepare for the worst. While it was not "easy" to hear, the medical foreshadowing allowed space for spiritual and emotional preparation. The distance between the suspected diagnosis and the actual results had given us the gift of time to begin processing what it means to watch decades of your life evaporate before your very eyes. In the following twenty-four hours we began sifting through our priorities, refocusing our lives, and reevaluating everything. We prayed for guidance and, amazingly, felt God's presence with us the entire time. Some people say they feel abandoned by God at times like this, and do not get me wrong, it is tough on your faith to get pummeled this hard out of the blue. However, rather than feeling abandoned, we felt as though God was in the room with us, holding us together.

And we sobbed. I do not mean we shed a few tears; I mean we held each other and sobbed. We cried over the grandchildren I would not see, and how I would miss their baptisms, graduations, and other key moments of their lives. How I would never walk my daughter down a long church aisle and see her begin a new life with someone she loved. Danelle and I wept over the years that were snatched from us in one crucial moment. How all of our plans of growing old together were suddenly just a dream. We are still crying sometimes, in the midst of trying to recover some sense of normalcy and while making sarcastic jokes about cancer, the shortness of life, and the irony of what I did on my summer vacation.

On Wednesday night, after what felt like an interminable wait, the diagnosis was confirmed. I have neuroendocrine tumors. However, when I received the diagnosis it was not this clear. So many medical words were thrown out so fast that my wife and I (both humanities people) had to scribble them down. Words like adenocarcinoma, neoplasm, metastasized, peri-pancreatic, etc. The gastrointestinal specialist who delivered the official diagnosis had an unusual accent which made it very difficult to understand all the long, complicated, medical terms. He said I'd have to stay until I had an oncology consult the next day and that perhaps I could be discharged by noon on Thursday. Suddenly the brevity of life was pressing and the idea of wasting another day to see a doctor who would have nothing to do with my treatment seemed like an intolerable waste. Time was precious and I was ready to seize every moment outside of that little room.

Whenever you hear the words "pancreatic" and "cancer" in the same sentence, red lights should start flashing and alarms should start blaring. A quick look at the American Cancer Association website confirmed that most patients who have a diagnosis of pancreatic cancer live three to six months. My head, still struggling to overcome the effects of painkillers, was spinning. I had a million questions, and a million things to do. I had to get out of this room, get somewhere normal, and make sure I had a plan to ensure my family was taken care of without me. I did not have time to wait around to talk to a cancer doctor that I'd never see again. What new thing was he going to tell me? That I was dying? I got that. Check. Time to move on.

The cloud of despair Danelle and I had been valiantly trying to hold at bay since Sunday suddenly filled the room with full force. Like a scene from the last Harry Potter movie, "death eaters" stormed our life's cozy castle, and suddenly we saw our hallowed walls of hope begin to crumble before us.

After the doctor left, a young and extremely capable nurse named Stephanie slipped into our room without cart or chart and just stood next to the wall. To this day, I know that God placed her on this floor at this moment for us. She was technically off the clock and was only covering until the assigned nurse could make it in. She had been the one to take the biopsy report, she had been the one to make sure we knew, and now she was standing in our room to make sure we understood what the doctor had told us. She explained the terms and spelled out the medical terminology so Danelle could write it all down to look up later. We then began to ask if the attending doctor would be up soon. We wanted to leave. I even told her that we would be leaving tomorrow morning AMA (against medical advice) if necessary, because I wanted to go home.

Sometimes you can see the light go on in somebody else's eyes. An idea occurs to them as if whispered by a divine source. Stephanie realized that there was no reason the oncologist we needed to see next needed to be in Erie. We would not be getting treatment here. We would be headed back to North Carolina, home of some of the preeminent medical facilities in the world. She indicated that she was going to contact the attending physician and see what she could do. There were many saints at St. Vincent who made our horrible stay bearable. Stephanie remains my angel.

As she left to begin trying to find a way for us to be discharged, we looked at our list of people to call. Ever since that day I have often remarked that the only thing worse than being told you have terminal cancer is having to call people and tell them that you have terminal cancer.

"Hi honey, it's Dad. How's it going? Oh me? Not so good, I have terminal cancer." No, that is not what I said, but that is what it felt like. Calling your children and telling them that you are dying is one of the toughest things you will ever do because you know that you are inflicting pain. You are not there to comfort them and let them cry in your arms. I knew my daughter Lydia had been waiting days, and she kept asking and kept asking and kept asking. She knew it was going to be bad. She is extremely, sometimes frighteningly, intuitive. She reads every vocal inflection, every word or change of words; she is like some sort of empathetic Jedi. She knew it, we confirmed it, and it broke her heart.

I hung up the phone and just sobbed. But that was just the beginning of the calls we had to make. I made one to my sister who, fifteen years older than me, was more like my mom growing up. She agreed to tell my brothers. Then I called my best friend to control the vocational/pastoral rumor mill. If you think ladies in a beauty parlor gossip, you ought to hear a bunch of pastors together.

Finally, I bailed. I was an emotionally exhausted, highly medicated introvert who had just laid my life out before so many people. I had to let Danelle take over.

Our calls to family and friends were interrupted by the arrival of the attending doctor who did a cursory exam and told us we could be discharged shortly, as long as we signed a form indicating that we would follow up with my primary care physician for a referral to an oncologist by Friday. We agreed. I had already contacted my doctor and had the wheels rolling. The doctor issued the discharge orders around 7 pm. The nurses' station went into action as the unit secretary began flinging charts and making copies. It became the mission of the team to get me out of the hospital and on the way home that night. I have never seen a group of medical professionals, or any group of professionals, work with such intensity. They were amazing. Danelle was sent to the pharmacy for prescriptions, paperwork was completed, copies made, and a DVD of all the pictures from my sonogram and CT scans was produced. IV lines were removed and discharge orders given.

While the medical team was buzzing, Danelle was continuing to make calls. I have no idea how many she made to relatives, friends, and family. She was brilliant, delivering very difficult news calmly, spelling out the terms, and being medically vague about the amount of time I was expected to live (we are quick learners).

About 10 pm on Wednesday, July 10, 2013 we made our way out of St. Vincent to start a new chapter in our lives. That was my "summer vacation."

***

So often in our lives it is easy to believe that people are the center of their own universe and do not really care for others. My "summer vacation" redeemed my belief in humanity. Over and over I saw the "kindness of strangers." People I did not know did extraordinary things to help me through a difficult time. From the very straightforward doctor who help prepare us for the worst to the patient care assistant who prayed for me every night while she took my vitals, the goodness in humanity showed up over and over again. The very image of God was displayed in simple but profound acts of kindness.

On our last evening I also saw how one person who decides to make a difference can motivate others. Stephanie saw our need and decided that she could help. Not only did she help but she garnered the assistance of her entire team including the attending physician. She convinced the unit secretary to stay a few minutes late to complete discharge papers, contacted the doctor to get them signed, and found a way to get us on our way when she could have just punched out and gone home.

How many times in our lives do we stand at the threshold of making a difference? We evaluate the options and decide whether we want to get involved or just turn a blind eye and head home. Daily, it seems, we face numerous chances to make somebody's life a little easier, even if it means ours may be a little more difficult. One of the commitments I am making is to be the stranger who serves. To seek out chances to make a difference. Will you?

Gracious God, thank You for the kindness of strangers You place in my life to help me through difficult times. Thank you that during the difficult times of my life You have promised never to abandon me but to go with me into the valley of the shadow of death. Help me to be the stranger who helps and not turn blind eyes to opportunities to bless others. In the name of the Great Shepherd who will never forsake me I pray. Amen.

Chapter 2 Cheeseburgers

"You can find something truly important in an ordinary minute."
Mitch Albom, author

Notice how the lilies grow. They do not wear themselves out with work, and they do not spin cloth. But I say to you that even Solomon in all his splendor wasn't dressed like one of these. Luke 12:27

There is a saying that even when they are only "pretty good" pizza, cheeseburgers, and sex are still awesome. I believe every facet of that saying. Do not get excited, I am not going to talk about sex, at least not today, but I am going to talk about cheeseburgers.

I like all types of cheeseburgers. I arrange meetings to be near good cheeseburger joints. I like the ones at Central Café, a local diner in Rocky Mount, North Carolina. The cheeseburgers there are pressed flat and served on a little, fluffy bun with chili and mustard. I also like big, thick bacon cheeseburgers from Red Robin with jalapeño medallions added just to spice things up. I love those little cheeseburger pieces of heaven at Five Guys, which are served with hand cut fries that you cannot quite finish alone. I like to make cheeseburgers from my own recipe and watch people eat them and be surprised that a burger can, sometimes, be as good as a steak. It is my contention that cheeseburgers will be on the heavenly banquet beside really good fried chicken and banana pudding. I will let you know when I get there.

So we were on our way to the car leaving the hospital. Danelle had successfully navigated a late night encounter with a panhandler at the local Rite Aid and was grateful when one of the parking valets at the hospital insisted she leave the car right by the door so I would not have to wait when we came back downstairs so late at night. She returned to the eighth floor, breathless, to take me home. We gathered documents, the infamous DVD with all the pictures of my guts, the clothes that had accumulated from camping in the hospital for four days and got on the elevator. I was still really shaky and the drop of the elevator felt a little like Disney's Tower of Terror, but the doors slid open and we made our way toward the parking lot.

The exterior doors opened and I felt the rush of cool, lake saturated summer air. After days of conditioned air filled with clinical smells, it almost took my breath away. The wind was blowing and I began to get chilled. Thanks to the valet guys, our car was nearby so I got into the passenger seat (a new experience for me actually), and we eased out of the driveway.

Now up until this point, my encounter with solid food since Saturday afternoon had mostly been in the wrong direction. While in the hospital the closest thing I had to real food was a couple of bagels Danelle had snuck in from Panera Bread Company with their amazing cream cheese (because the hospital's bagels as I previously mentioned, were like hockey pucks) and some bland chicken noodle soup. I needed something on my stomach in order to take my evening pain medication and Danelle asked what I wanted. You guessed it; I said, "I want a cheeseburger." I had to convince Danelle that my first meal since being sprung from the joint should be a McDonald's double cheeseburger with a small chocolate shake. Later she said she was convinced that I would be revisiting that meal. It is not exactly the "healthy choice" you know, but what the heck, I am dying anyway.

We pulled into the drive-thru and made the order, only after Danelle checked at least two more times to make sure that is what I wanted. The teenager at the window handed us the bag and the cup. Those first few sips of cold milkshake bathed the back of my throat and re-awakened my taste buds. I had wondered if they would ever come back to life after hospital food. Then I took a bite of the burger.

One of the side effects I am having is that sometimes I am really hungry and may not know it. It may be pressure in my abdomen or the fact that I was NPO (no food or drink) for two days, but my stomach has a tough time sending messages to my brain. I took that first bite of a completely average cheeseburger and it tasted…normal. It did not taste like the best thing I had ever eaten, it was not incredible, but it was predictable. At that moment some sense of normalcy re-entered my topsy-turvy world. A little of the fog lifted as I began to realize that in the middle of the storm of my life, the rest of the world kept turning. I took another bite, and another. I had to force myself to slow down because I also realized, for the first time in days, that I was incredibly hungry. I ate some of Danelle's fries, drank some more shake, and finished the burger. Part of life had been set right by a cheap cheeseburger. Who knew?

***

We undervalue the mundane. Maybe you do not, but I know I have. I have often grown bored with the daily grind of life. The predictable things like mortgage payments, cooking supper, and mowing the grass (all right, I am busted, I pay somebody to cut my grass) seem like drudgery. That night, eating that completely average cheeseburger I understood the value of the predictable in my life. I understood how mundane rhythms are really God's way of helping us have a foundation for our lives.

You have to be careful upon what you build your life's

foundation. You have to be selective about what normal things you seek to incorporate into your life. Sure, you have to go to work, do the chores, pay the bills. There are some things that you need to choose to include in your regular rhythms. We all need to include times of rest and reflection. We need dedicated time to love deeply those in our lives who mean the most to us. We need to remember to live passionately and follow our hearts. We need to find a way to listen to God and nurture our soul. Sometimes those things feel like drudgery too. You think you are just going through the motions, that you are not really "getting anything out of it." So what? Keep doing it. Keep spending that intentional time with those you love, pursuing God, and seeking your life's purpose. It is worth it!

Include simple rituals in your life like engaging in spiritual reading before your feet hit the floor, saying your favorite prayer at lunchtime, or talking for fifteen minutes with your spouse before you drift off to sleep. Keep practicing those simple, everyday disciplines because in one moment, the ordinary can slip away. When it returns it renews your soul. There may be a day in your life when everything falls apart. Oh sure, you may not get diagnosed with inoperable, terminal cancer; you may have a car accident, lose a loved one, or find yourself at the end of your rope. It is at those times when you are going to long for the days when the world was normal. When you return to those things, you will realize you should never undervalue the mundane again.

One day you are going to wish you just had a cheeseburger.

God, I confess that I have sinned by not appreciating the places You show up in the mundane things of life. Thank You for making me more aware of how important simple things like paying the bills, cheeseburgers, and cooking supper bring balance to my life, which is so often out of control. In the name of the One who has the whole world in His hands, Jesus, I pray. Amen

Chapter 3 The Shower of Power

*"Reflect on your present blessings, of which every man has many,
not on your past misfortunes, of which all men have some."*
Charles Dickens, writer

*But God can also turn the desert into watery pools, thirsty ground into watery
springs.* Psalm 107:35

It is amazing how far a couple of hundred feet is when you
have not walked for days. When we finally arrived at our friend
Diane's home, which was where Danelle was staying while I was in
the hospital, I am sure I looked a lot like the "little old man" always
depicted by Tim Conway on the old *Carol Burnett Show,* shuffling
along the sidewalk, careful not to fall. I climbed the four steps to
the porch, holding onto Danelle's shoulder for stability and entered
the house.

It smelled like somebody's home. No more clinical
disinfectant, just that clean smell of lemony Pledge and home
cooking. I shuffled to the bedroom while Danelle gathered my
toiletries and put them in the shower. It dawned on me that, with
the exception of the occasional sponge bath, I had not really
showered since Sunday morning…gross!

The shower in Diane's home was gorgeous, like something

from a magazine: river rock floor, beautiful ceramic tiles, duel spray heads cascading warm water. I turned the water on and entered the glass doors. For long minutes I just stood there, water running down my face.

There is nothing like a hot shower on a tough day. It seems to not only wash away the grunge from your body, but also the stains on your soul. I think that is because it intuitively reminds those of us who are Christians of our baptism. How that simple act of ritual washing symbolized the removal of the stain of sin on our souls. The water refreshes, renews, and restores life.

That night in that shower, tears mixed with the soapy water as the pent up emotions of the previous few days washed over me like a tidal wave. This was the first moment when I fully realized that I was journeying through what the psalmist calls "the valley of the shadow of death." My soul seemed empty and all I had left was a cry of lament, imploring God to hold me up when my strength failed.

Faith is a difficult thing to describe. It sometimes seems when you need it most, you possess it least. That night as the reality that my life had radically changed set in. All I had was a small glimmer of hope left. So I wept.

Danelle says men are horrible criers because we do not get enough practice. I am sure she is right; I really stink at this whole crying thing. But there are times when you do not care whether you are good at it or not, it just has to come out. When I was at East Carolina University's School of Social Work, one of my clinical advisors used to say about clients crying, "simply remind them that tears on the outside wash away; tears trapped on the inside stay and stay." I am not sure I ever fully understood this concept until that night.

Somehow the waters of the shower mixed with my tears seemed to wash away some of the anxiety and fear. They cleared out some of the disappointment at everything I would miss and seemed to affirm the voice of God in my heart that my wife would be loved and my family cared for even in my absence.

I finally turned off the water as my fingers began to wrinkle. I took my evening meds, shuffled to the bedroom where my beloved wife tucked me in like you would a small child. I lay on the side that did not cause pain and began to pray the centering prayer I have taught so many others as a place of solace in difficult times, "Lord Jesus, Son of God, have mercy on me, a sinner."

Somewhere in the night my prayers were heard and I fell into a deep sleep that would not be interrupted by IV alarms, the need to take vital signs, or someone from the lab coming to take more blood. I could finally rest because God assured me that He had it under control that night and I could just let it all go…and I did. At least for a few hours.

***

There is power in having a strategy prepared when you face times and situations beyond your control. Centering prayer, also called mindfulness, is one of those strategies that I have found particularly helpful. Whether I'm entering an MRI machine and having to lie still for an hour, or I am suffering from insomnia, centering prayer allows me to be fully present in the midst of the tidal wave of emotions and the depths of worry that sometimes seem overwhelming. A combination of breathing exercises, words with deep meaning, and a mental image to focus upon, this practice has been shown to reduce blood pressure, ease anxiety, and lower stress. What is your strategy to deal with things when your world is out of control?

Gracious God, you remind me with every shower that your forgiveness washes away the trials and transgressions of my life. I know that when I cry, You cry with me, that You are present in the darkest places of my life to shed the light of hope upon me. Thank You, Jesus, for going with me into the valley of the shadow of death. Amen.

Chapter 4 The Long Drive Home

"The strength of a nation is derived from the integrity of its homes."
Confucius, philosopher

Your word is a lamp before my feet and a light for my journey.
Psalm 119:105

There's no place like home...

After a night of codeine-enhanced dreams (once I was melting sand, and another time I dreamt I was in a Native American sweat lodge), I woke up at 5:00 a.m. Now normally that would be early, but having slept most of seven hours in a row for the first time since Saturday night, I felt almost human. I still had that post-hospital, highly medicated fog, but clarity and consciousness were slowly re-entering my brain.

Danelle and I got up, got dressed and made our way to Panera Bread Company for breakfast. After I got my coffee infusion and Danelle received her minimum daily allowance of peanut butter and Diet Pepsi, we got on the road. Since Danelle would be doing all of the driving, the goal for the day was to drive five or six of the almost eleven hour drive. We figured that would put us more than halfway home but not wear her down any further than the hospital ordeal already had.

You should also know that Danelle Cauley, the love of my life, is my hero. When you meet her, she comes off as a high-energy bundle of joy; but what you do not see is the spiritual and emotional superhero that lies underneath. If my faith has stayed strong, it's because her spirit has supported me. When doubt has crept into my soul, she has held the candle of hope to help me find the way back out. When I have been racked with sobs, she has held me and cried with me. When I was emotionally spent after just three phone calls (being a true introvert when dealing with people one-on-one), she picked up the phone and called literally dozens more people. She has graciously handled calls from our beloved Bishop Hope Morgan Ward, spoke to my District Superintendent, and fielded calls from friends, relatives, and church members. If Superwoman has a secret identity, I am sure it is Danelle Cauley. One of her sisters got it right when they told her that she was the "strongest of the bunch." Were it not for her, there is a fair chance I would be curled up in a corner, waiting to die. She gives me a million reasons to live!

During our long car ride home, Danelle and I talked about everything and nothing. We skirted around the difficult stuff because we did not want to have to pull over on the Pennsylvania Turnpike and bawl our eyes out. (I can just see it now, "No officer we're fine, we just needed to pull over and cry for a while. We are fine to continue on…"). We talked about going to Disney, about getting some home projects done so they would not be hanging over my head, and about what to have for lunch. Like I said about cheeseburgers, never undervalue the mundane; it gives you something to retreat to when your world falls apart.

We stopped for lunch at *Bob Evans*, not normally my pick, but I knew they would have comfort food. Sure enough, chicken pot pie in the middle of summer was just what I needed to start putting some color back in my cheeks. Conversation was light over lunch as Danelle fielded another five or six phone calls. I was still not quite ready to talk to a lot of people. Thank God for text messages that allow you to reach out and communicate without having to speak.

After lunch Danelle felt somewhat renewed and decided to drive a couple of more hours to get to somewhere nicer to stay for the evening. We were hoping for an upgrade from the truck stop motels that were in the immediate vicinity. We wanted something with interior hallways, soft sheets, and without the smell of diesel fuel.

Having abandoned the turnpike for the rolling hills of Virginia, we were weaving our way through small towns, past vineyards, and across farm country when another number showed up on my phone. When I answered, it was a physician's liaison from the Duke Cancer Center. My primary care physician back home had finally seen all of my reports, and got on the phone to help us get seen as quickly as possible. The woman on the other end of the line asked "Can you make it to the Duke Cancer Center tomorrow morning at 8:00 a.m?" Without hesitation Danelle said, "Tell her yes."

In all the years of our marriage, Danelle had never driven more than five hours in a row unassisted. She has made the trip to our mountain home or back a time or two, but she avoided making the journey alone and driving the whole way at all costs. Now my Superwoman wife was ready to finish out an eleven-hour trip and then turn around and drive another couple of hours in the morning to get me to the Duke Cancer Center. We eventually pulled over and had a somewhat extensive conversation with the physician's liaison laying out the types of tumors I had, how long I had had the diagnosis (20 hours at this point), and what I needed to bring with me the next day. Along with being a spiritual and emotional powerhouse, Danelle might be the most organized person I know. She made a list and checked it twice. She was going to get this whole treatment ball rolling if she had to push it herself. My discharge packet became precious cargo, and the DVD with all the pictures of my scans was treated like a top-secret package for the president. Her mission was clear and you bet she accepted it.

From this point on Danelle drove with one objective in mind: get us home. We stopped only to get out, re-caffeinate, go to the restroom, and walk around so she could wake up from hours of highway driving on I-95. God was with us because there were no real significant tie-ups, not even around Richmond. Finally we pulled off the highway and made our way home.

As we pulled into the driveway, all I could think of were the famous words of Dorothy from the *Wizard of Oz,* "There's no place like home. There's no place like home. There's no place like home." If you have ever been away from home for an extended period of time, you know there is something spiritual about opening the door and feeling like you are back in your "place."

I have never been so happy to sit at my kitchen counter, eat take out, and just be home. That night we spent time with our young adult daughter, Lydia, who was living with us while she attended graduate school. We explained all we knew up to that point, cried some more (good thing we buy Kleenex© at Sam's Club), and laughed until our sides hurt. We made sarcastic cancer jokes. I decided I am going to buy a t-shirt that says, "I am Not Dead Yet" (quote from Monty Python movie) to remind people of my status. Never in my life has my bed felt so good. Just to be home, in my place, somehow put the world back into some sense of order. Yes, my pillow was wet with tears, but they were tears of both sadness and joy on that evening because I was home.

***

It does not really matter whether it is a shanty or a palace; your place restores your soul. Your home is where you can hide from the world. Your place is where there are people who love you, even if you leave laundry on the floor and have not shaved for days. I understood something that evening that I have known all along, but like so many of life's lessons it became even more precious. We are a people who need a place. That is why I like the translation of that famous scripture, "My Father's house has room to spare…I am going to prepare a place for you…" (Common English Bible, John 14). We are a people who need a place.

Where is your place? Do you really value and appreciate your place or are you always dissatisfied and looking for the next place? Do not get me wrong, I have a long list of things I would like to do to my "place," but I also appreciate just having a spot in the universe where I can retreat from the world, where I can meet God and be angry with Him over cancer, and where I give Him thanks for the joys of my life. There is no place like home.

Gracious God, I am ever thankful that You have given me this place with these people. Help me to remember to focus on how blessed I am, and to give You thanks for simple things, like having a home. In the name of the One who prepares my next home, Jesus, I pray, Amen

Chapter 5 An Environment of Hope

"There are no hopeless situations; there are only
men who have grown hopeless about them."
Clare Booth Luce, playwright

Endurance produces character, and character produces hope. Romans 5:4

When Friday morning dawned, I was feeling very surreal. It was as if I was awakening from a dream or seeing life through a frosted filter. I was home but my world had shifted off its axis. Everything looked the same. The raised bed garden needed tending (it still does), the deck had not magically finished itself, and there was a big stack of mail to sort. Even though for us it seemed that time had frozen during the past week, for the rest of the world it was business as usual.

The good news was that I was home in my own bed (thank you *The Original Mattress Factory,* the best money I have ever spent), with normal smells and sounds. The bad news was that I was experiencing new symptoms like night sweats (which are very unpleasant).

That morning I awoke before the 5:00 a.m. alarm. Danelle and I got ready to go the Duke Cancer Center. After eating a quick breakfast and having coffee made from freshly ground beans we rolled out the door by 6:00 a.m.

When speaking with the physician's liaison the previous day she had told us to pack bags in case Duke wanted to keep me overnight. Just packing the bag with the potential of not coming back to my "place" that morning made me nauseated. If I have learned anything, it is that it is easier to face anything as long as you can make it home at the end of the day. I warned Danelle that if they wanted to keep me it may just be the straw that broke the camel's back and I might very well break down.

We drove what I knew would become a very familiar path, Highway 64 West to 540 West, to Durham. We pulled up in front of the Duke Cancer Center about 7:30 a.m. We were pleasantly surprised to see valet parking because finding parking at Duke is akin to winning the lottery. Plus I was still a little unstable on my feet and the long walk from the garage to the hospital might have been too taxing.

We walked into the mammoth lobby and were immediately greeted by an older man who noticed our bewilderment. He asked where we were going and we told him our destination. He then guided us to the elevator, led us up to the third floor, pointed out the restrooms, and showed us where we would check in at 8 a.m. It was the first time I have ever experienced such hospitality from a hospital. It was more like entering a fine hotel, complete with concierge service and fresh baked muffins, than a medical facility.

The waiting area itself surrounds a multi-floor entryway that has beautiful art in lovely colors. Its architectural features, like wood-framed finishing, are reminiscent of the windows of Duke Chapel. On the ground floor is an amazing piece of tile art that is filled with quotes related to hope. If there has ever been a building designed to inspire hope, it is the Duke Cancer Center.

We eventually signed in and were handed a clipboard with a form on it to complete about pain level and basic personal information as well as what resembled a restaurant pager. We sat at a small, wooden café table and completed the form while making small talk about how lovely the building was.

After spending days during the first part of the week in clean but very clinical surroundings, I cannot tell you how much I appreciated being somewhere that felt hopeful. Oh, I can imagine the conversations that must have arisen over the extravagance of the architecture, but I thank God that in this case the artists had a voice over the pragmatists. There is something about entering the building that lets you know, "this is where the best of the best come and give people a big dose of hope to go with their chemo, radiation, and medicine."

A few minutes before our appointed time our buzzer went off and we were escorted back into the "inner sanctum." I was measured, weighed, and had my vitals checked (a pattern I was becoming accustomed to), and we were assigned an examination room. What a great room! In the center of the room is what appears to be a throne with a soft seat and armrests and a high, padded back. You eventually realize it is also the exam table that rises from the floor and can lay back to make the patient supine for an examination. The room is more spacious than a typical exam room with extra seating available for family and an efficient workstation. The first bubbly young woman entered and began gathering essential information, asking if we needed something to drink or eat while we waited. She came across more like a hostess than a medical professional. Then our nurse came in, a sturdy woman with a European accent and took medical history.

"This is all the medicine you take?"

"Yes."

"No symptoms before Sunday?"

"No."

"Well you are an overachiever, Dr. Cauley. I can't think of anyone I have ever seen who was diagnosed on Wednesday and here on Friday."

I think that was her attempt at humor. She was professional, efficient, and obviously experienced. When she came across the pain meds that the hospital had given me, she clicked her tongue in disapproval that they would give something with Tylenol to somebody who had liver issues. "We will have to take care of that," she pronounced with authority.

Next came Dr. Harder. We later learned that he was a Navy physician who was training with our oncologist in gastrointestinal oncology as his specialty. He was an amazing listener. Danelle and I took turns relating the story of our vacation. A couple of days in Berkeley Springs, a roller coaster ride, the family party, the discomfort that turned into pain that turned into an attack requiring an Emergency Room visit. I laid out my pain-med-enhanced version of the hospital stay and Danelle filled in the gaps that I had missed. Then, the questions:

"Night sweats?"

"Well not really until last night."

"Reflux?"

"Yes but I've been taking Prilosec for years."

"Flushing? Hot flashes?"

"Nope."

"So no real symptoms until Sunday morning?"

Get the feeling there is a trend in these questions? Sometimes it felt like a very polite police interrogation and that they were looking for any inconsistency between stories or to see if any new revelations arose. I would later learn that this practice is intentional to see if any new revelations arise or inconsistencies are noted between the stories. The truth, it seems, is usually quite consistent. Inconsistencies indicate that the patient may not be telling the "whole truth," omitting things that may be determined to be unfavorable.

The doctor listened to my lungs (figured out later they were trying to see if I had decreased lung function), pushed on my abdomen (still a little tender), and felt my glands. Everything seemed normal, except for that whole cancer-in-my-liver thing, I mean. Before he left, he indicated that he and the senior oncologist were going to review the film, biopsy report, blood work, etc. from St. Vincent and they would be back in a few minutes.

He stepped out of the room and Danelle and I just sat there, still in that state where you know what is happening but you keep thinking, "This can't be happening." The funny thing about being sick, especially with a time-sensitive illness like cancer, is that you spend a lot of time waiting. I generally do not wait well, but I am learning to be comfortable just waiting.

Dr. Hope Uronis blew into the room like a whirlwind. A thin, small-framed woman who exudes confidence (and who would rather be called Hope than Dr. Uronis), she had the appearance of a marathon runner.

"How are you feeling?"

At that question Danelle and I burst out laughing,

"Oh I know!" Dr. Hope said, "It just comes out."

Danelle and I had been experimenting with creative ways to answer the, "How are you feeling?" question. This time I answered, "Like used gum on the bottom of an elephant's foot walking thru a dung pile." I thought that was pretty accurate at the moment.

Together, we reviewed the history again to verify everything: no symptoms, pain level, started Sunday, diagnosed on Wednesday, etc. Dr. Hope listened to my chest, poked on my abdomen, and felt my glands

"Well, it's not pancreatic cancer in the traditional sense," she announced. "What you have are neuroendocrine tumors (NETs). This is a set of slow growing tumors that have metastasized to your liver and perhaps other places. We will need an octreotide scan and another CT scan to determine more about the state of the metastases." Danelle was writing furiously while I sat on the exam throne and listened as if in a fog.

We then asked the big question: how long? Will I be able to go to the Masquerade Ball in October? "Oh, that shouldn't be a problem," she told us. But then she went into the frustratingly vague medical language. "We can't really know until we have more time points and understand how fast it is growing," "It is of indeterminate origin." Then she said, "You should have many, many months."

When you are thinking you have six weeks to three months to live, "many months" seems like an eternity. Those words came as a huge relief that I wasn't going to abandon those I love so quickly. Danelle said it was like a band of pressure lifted off her head hearing those words, "many months." I know if I walked up to you in the street and said you had "many months" to live, you'd probably panic (or think I was insane). But all I could think about was the music video, *Savin' Me* by Nickelback where there are clocks over everyone's head counting down the years, months, days, hours, minutes, and seconds they have left to live. At that moment I really wanted to see my "life clock" so I could make the most of the time I had left.

We left the exam room and headed down to schedule additional scans and to get more labs. I believe I had more blood drawn in that one week than all of my life up to that point. Funny thing, all my blood work came back within acceptable levels. No red flags. Actually, my labs were all better than they had been a couple of years earlier. These would be the same, all coming back within normal range for a healthy, adult male of 48. Essentially, I am healthy as a horse, except for the whole cancer thing.

Finally we exited the Duke Cancer Center with a great sense of relief and a lot more questions. The octreotide scan and CT scan were scheduled for July 23 & 24. We would see Dr. Hope again on Monday, July 29th to get the results. More waiting. More wondering. More making wish lists of what we want to do together during our "many months."

We were told to "return to normal"—whatever that means—as much as possible. I could go back to the gym, but take it easy for a few weeks. I was cleared go back to work on light duty for a couple of weeks, then to do as much as I could tolerate. I was given better pain meds, told to abandon Tylenol and use ibuprofen three times a day on a regular basis to control ongoing discomfort, and sent back to my "normal life." All of this before lunchtime.

With our new lease on life, we picked up the car and I got behind the wheel for the first time since Sunday morning, five days previous. We headed to *Macaroni Grill* to celebrate having "many months" instead of just a few weeks. Not long after we navigated off the Duke campus I looked over and Danelle was asleep; I mean really asleep. I have a picture but I am forbidden to share it. With the band of concern lifted from her head and the immediate need to "be strong" gone, the week's exhaustion settled in and took over for the thirty-minute ride from Durham to Raleigh. It was the first time she looked relaxed in days.

After lunch we made our way home. We gave Lydia the update and headed for a nap; a nap that would last for three hours. All of the week's weariness had sapped our bodies, minds, and souls of all reserves. We lay down on the bed and within minutes were fast asleep. Everything looks better after a nap.

***

Time is precious. We talk about living every day to the fullest, but usually live most days like we have an endless supply. Mortality is an interesting thing. We all give intellectual acquiescence to the idea of our mortality, but live as though we are really immortal. I understand why. If we are not careful, we allow the urgent to overwhelm the important when we assume that we can always make up for today by borrowing on our tomorrows. We leverage the future by sacrificing the joy of the present.

So what am I doing with my new knowledge that I have "many months" to live? I am making lists and setting goals. I am setting twelve-month goals, eighteen-month goals, twenty-four month goals, and thirty-six month goals. These are simple things: I want to see my second grandchild who is due January 1, 2014; I want to go to Disney World and suspend reality for several days; I want to turn 49 (and 50, and 51...); I want to see my daughter, Lydia, graduate from Duke Divinity School and my stepson, Jacob, graduate from high school. I want to do more baptisms, marry a few more couples who are really in love, even do more funerals because I really understand how precious life is. I want to live every minute as if it were my last. I want to sit on the beach and watch the sun come up; I want to drink really good wine; I want to eat really good food; I want to laugh with friends until we cry, and cry with friends until we laugh. I want to live my many, many months so that when I die, I can slide into heaven and say, "Whew, what a rush! Hey, God, what's next?" At the risk of sounding like a country song, I am going live like I am dying, because I am; and just so we are clear, you are too. And, I am going to live with hope.

God I confess that there are days when I am completely without hope, days that I have let doubt overwhelm me. Thank You for sending people who restore my hope and who believe for me when I have no faith left. Thank You for the gift of sunrises that remind me that with each new day, new hope can arise. In the name of the hope giver, Jesus, I pray. Amen.

PS. Both my oncologist and my presiding bishop are named Hope. I am surrounded by Hope!

Chapter 6 Surreal Saturday

"Courage is the price life exacts for granting peace."
Amelia Earhart, aviator

It's necessary for this rotting body to be clothed with what can't decay, and the body that is dying to be clothed in what can't die. 1 Corinthians 15:53

We "slept in" on Saturday. For the Cauleys, that means we managed to sleep until 8:00 a.m. We were determined to salvage one day of vacation. We ate breakfast and decided to get out of town before too many people knew we were back. I was not in the mood to entertain too many visitors. At the end of the day I am pretty much an introvert. I have always said I would rather be on the platform than in the congregation any day. At parties it is Danelle who makes the small talk; usually I just smile and nod. Now, with the overwhelming news of a terminal illness, I was not ready to have people come over to our house and look at me "that way." You know what I mean? People would begin to look at me with those sad eyes and then apologize for my being sick. I am sick, it sucks, now let's get on with living.

By 2:00 p.m. we were having lunch in Raleigh at *Red Robin*. As previously mentioned, I love cheeseburgers. I especially love Red Robin cheeseburgers. There is a reason that whenever you say

Red Robin, somebody will say, "Yum!" and it is not just because of great commercials. You just can not beat a slab of meat, melted cheese, thick bacon, and all the fixings on a fluffy bun.

I was halfway through the burger before I realized it did not have any flavor. Oh, I am sure it tasted awesome, it is just I seemed to be unable to taste. It was as if somebody turned off my taste buds. The rest of the day followed suit. We shopped for a hot tub to replace the one that was damaged in the hurricane more than a year ago. One of the recommendations for my condition was to do anything that would relieve tension, help me relax, and reduce stress hormones. We went and saw a movie that was somewhat entertaining, but it really did not hold my interest. The whole day I was distracted and disinterested. It was as if life itself had lost its flavor, like I was watching the world in black and white with no color. I learned later that I was experiencing a mild form of what psychologists call emotional trauma.

When you experience something that happens unexpectedly, something for which you are completely unprepared, and something you are powerless to prevent, it causes psychological and emotional distress. There are a myriad of vague symptoms like irritability, inability to concentrate, not enjoying things that normally give you pleasure (like cheeseburgers!), edginess, tension, anxiety, etc. You essentially withdraw inward as you try to understand how something so random could happen to you.

It is funny; having been trained as a social worker makes it fascinating to evaluate what is happening on your inside from the outside. I had been given news that was personally devastating and, even worse, devastating to those I loved. I had not yet had serious symptoms, with the exception of some residual soreness and some stiffness from having spent several days in the hospital. While I knew intellectually I was dying, physically I was recovering rather quickly. I was having a hard time conceiving the magnitude of the situation. It was bigger than anything I had ever faced. This was the big one, the one that would kill me. This was life and death.

That evening as I was preparing what I would share with Saint Paul United Methodist Church the next morning. I came across this Scripture from James 4:13-15: *"Now listen, you who say, 'Today or tomorrow we will go to this or that city, spend a year there, carry on business and make money.' Why, you do not even know what will happen tomorrow. What is your life? You are a mist that appears for a little while and then vanishes. Instead, you ought to say, 'If it is the Lord's will, we will live and do this or that.'"* With this, some of the fog that was hovering around my soul lifted. I realized that, in essence, I am just like everyone else except I have a much greater awareness of my mortality. All of our lives are just a "mist," some of us are just more aware of it than others.

It is rather surreal to look into the mirror of your own mortality. Largely I am happy with what I have done with my life. Oh, sure, there are things I would change, mistakes I have made that I would like to undo, but by and large I have lived my life by giving it away and investing in other people and in things eternal. I have done my very best to serve struggling local churches, help people come to know Christ, disciple them into being radical believers, and release them to live out their divine calling. I got to spend five years as the Director of Ministry with Young People at Lake Junaluska, a conference center in the mountains of North Carolina. I spent that time mentoring some amazing young adults and leading youth events where literally thousands of young people made first time professions of faith or rededicated their lives to Christ. I have raised more than $70,000 to help ZOE Ministry mentor orphans in Africa. I have been lucky enough to design events to train clergy and laity in evangelism and discipleship, help youth embrace missions, and even help my wife start a non-profit theatre company. Looking back I can say that I have loved deeply, lived passionately, and sought to listen to God intentionally and do what He has led me to do. What more could I ask?

***

The mirror of mortality makes a lot of things very clear. It becomes obvious what things really are not worth the very limited days you have left. Petty grievances and little disagreements just are not worth the limited emotional energy I have left. I have always been surprised at the grudges people hold, the bitterness that they cling to, and the pain that almost seems to give them their identity. I do not understand those who see every glass as half-empty, every problem as insurmountable, and every little disagreement as an opportunity to complain. What a waste of precious life.

People treat you differently when you are dying. I have noticed that when people are around me they, too, are forced to look into the mirror of their own mortality. This makes some folks quite reflective and causes them to take stock of what they are holding onto that they need to release. It makes some people very uncomfortable because they realize that their days are numbered, just like mine, though my number might be lower. It makes them realize that if I am dying after spending two years getting healthier than I have been in two decades, they too must face the realization that, as James reminded us, their life is just a "mist." Maybe that is a gift I can give my friends and acquaintances, to help them remember to treat every day as a precious gift, every kiss as a treasure, and every embrace as a symbol of God's divine presence in the midst of life's ever present chaos.

I have come up with an answer for those who ask what they can do for me. I tell them: love deeply; live passionately; and listen intentionally to God, then do what He says. If you do that, when the day comes that you find yourself looking into the mirror of your own mortality, you will be happy with what you find.

Loving God, help me to love deeply, live passionately, and to listen to You intentionally and be willing to do whatever You ask so that when the day comes that I stand before You I will be ready to enter Your presence without regret. Help me to live so that I will be ready to die. In the name of the One who showed us how to live, Jesus, I pray. Amen.

Chapter 7 Telling 200 Of Your Friends You Have Cancer

"Nothing worth doing is completed in our lifetime;
therefore, we must be saved by hope."
Reinhold Niebuhr, theologian

Sing to the Lord, all the earth! Share the news of his saving work every single day! 1 Chronicles 16:23

At the risk of repeating myself, and I know it sounds ridiculous, but in some ways it is harder telling people you love that you have terminal cancer than hearing it for yourself. Oh, it sucks when the doctor tells you that you are probably going to die of cancer. Absorbing that punch to your soul is pretty tough, but you are the only person the doctor tells, you and whoever is with you at that moment. When you recover from that punch you realize that you have a couple of options. You can be stoic and try to go it alone. Be tough and not let anyone know. This is a horrible idea spiritually, personally, and psychologically. The other option is you can begin passing along the truthful information, first to those closest to you, and then to others. I have learned that no matter how carefully you put out the information, somebody will catastrophize an already bad situation and begin spreading wrong information. Thanks to the internet, everyone considers themselves an expert because Wikipedia is never wrong…LOL.

By Sunday we had made dozens of calls. In truth, I made very few calls; Danelle made most of them. By the third call she had a script memorized that gave the basic information we had in summary with key medical terms highlighted. She also had answers to the questions people would ask, "No we do not know how long he has to live;" "Yes it is terminal, yes that means he will probably die from it, that's what terminal means"; and "He is doing as well as can be expected" (which is code for "he is devastated but determined)."

We survived the barrage of calls and inquiries on Friday and Saturday, but there was still one more hurdle to jump: Sunday morning. Being a pastor means that every week you stand in front of a group of people and share God's story and occasionally snippets of your story. Part of what this means is that the people in the pew probably know you better than you will ever know all of them. They know about your youthful foolishness (like the time I crashed my uncle's tractor into the ditch), about the people who led you to faith, and about the people who have made a difference in your life. This also means that as a group their faith story is tied, however tenuously, to your faith story. By Friday I had determined that I needed to show up on Sunday morning to prove that the tales of my untimely demise had been greatly exaggerated and to let them know the truth to dispel as many rumors as possible.

Sunday morning dawned sunny and warm. I made the decision that we would slide in during the hymn before the message at the 9:00 a.m. traditional worship service so as not to disturb it too much. I did not want to endure the "Passing of the Peace," that awkward time where people shake hands and greet those around them. I knew my presence during this time would disrupt the worship service completely, plus I hate that part of the service (remember, I am an introvert). As we walked up the hall, we heard the final verses of the song, "We Are The Church." We slid into the back pew. The guest speaker preached a great sermon on forgiveness that closed with prayer. After the offering was received, Danelle and I made our way to the front to share with the congregation. Our 9:00 am service is made up mostly of senior adults who prefer traditional worship and hymns.

In all the classes I had attended in high school, college, graduate school, and my post-graduate work nobody ever taught me how to stand in front of a group of people and tell them I was dying. Because I serve a modest-sized, United Methodist congregation, that means there are a lot of people over the age of sixty-five in our normal attendance. Often I have heard them say that they have "served their time" and were too old to serve on committees. I usually remind them that according to the Bible, "if you are not dead, you are not done." That morning I used that line again.

"It's great to be back from what is, perhaps, the worst vacation ever. I stayed in a room that I am sure will turn out to be the least comfortable, and most expensive room I have every slept in for vacation in my life. It was at St. Vincent's Hospital in Erie, Pennsylvania."

I then went on to explain the bare essentials of my condition, that I would not be quitting work anytime soon because I intended to live until I died; I would be taking all of my vacation time in the next couple of years, unlike most previous years when I had barely taken any. Danelle went on to explain some of the more detailed medical information and respectfully requested that our house not be bombarded with guests for the next couple of weeks as we tried to find our rhythm.

I do not know if you attend a mainline church, but there is the tradition that the pastor stands at the back door and greets people as they leave. During these times, we unintentionally invite people to lie to us because they feel compelled to tell us how great that day's message was as they shake our hand.

At the end of the service I moved to the rear of the sanctuary to greet people as they left. On this day, my emotionally conservative senior congregation was overwhelmingly affectionate. Maybe because they, too, were close to the end of their days and they related with how suddenly life's brevity had become a reality in my life. Either way, on this day I received more hugs than handshakes and there were a lot of tears.

After we finished the receiving line I retreated into my office to recover before the 10:45 a.m. worship service. Remember, I am an introvert who had just spent a half hour explaining my terminal illness to seventy people and then had to greet almost every one of them as they looked at me like I was, well, dying. I mean, I know I am dying but when people look at you like you are dying, it is kind of depressing.

The later service was easier. The music is louder. The pace is faster. The congregation is younger. The whole environment is more casual. The previous day I had contacted my spiritual mentor, Dr. Laura Early, and she indicated that she might show up for the later worship service. Dr. Early sauntered in with her normal cowgirl swagger at 10:30 a.m. carrying several things in her hand. She planted herself right up front with Danelle and me and made herself at home.

At the end of Shawn's message, just like in the earlier service, Danelle and I stood up and went through the process again. We shared about my disease, how I planned to continue working as long as possible, and how our family needed some time to get used to this "new normal" and find our pace. About the time I was wrapping up, Dr. Early stood up. There are very few people in my life who are not only not intimidated by me, but intimidate me. This 5'4" woman has the ability to put me in my place with a single look. She stood up and said, "Honey, you can sit down."

She then looked at me and said something I completely did not expect. She said that I was like one of her children (Laura is a few years older than I am) and that if she could take my place and take the cancer from me, she would. The gravity of those words expressed an affection I am not sure I fully grasped up until that moment. For somebody to stand up in front of a group of people and tell you she loves you so dearly that she would die for you is incredibly humbling. Why would anyone be willing to die for me?

Laura began to talk to the congregation about my previous unwillingness to take time off. After reminding us that this was unhealthy and that she expected I would improve upon this in the future, she turned to look straight at me. She said, "That is a sin." My congregation watched as their pastor received a spiritual challenge in front of the whole church! And she is right; it is a sin to forget to rest and to Sabbath. It is a violation of the fourth commandment to press on without resting, thinking you are too invaluable to pause. Next she addressed some of the plans I had shared with the congregation such as wanting to write a book or two before I die. She reminded me to let God lead my time and said she was not convinced that books were what He might want from me right now. Yeah, she takes her job as my spiritual mentor seriously; I always tell people that Danelle and Laura are the two women in my life who can really tell me the hard truths.

Next Laura presented me with the several gifts. She had a book for Danelle and me to read about a medical doctor who died of cancer. She showed the church a little pin that she had felt led to purchase years ago when she was at Walt Disney World. It had been sitting on her dresser ever since. She said although she did not know why, even then God knew it would be for me, even before she did. It is a Disney pin that says "LOVE"; she had heard that I really wanted to take one last trip to Disney, and she wanted me to wear the pin to remind me how much I am loved.

Laura is one of the greatest United Methodist pastors I know; she works in the most impoverished community in North Carolina and does an amazing job bringing hope and shining light into the world. She is also seriously resistant to technology and will even admit that her dear husband prints off her emails so she can read them like letters. What she said next let me know just how much she loves me; she told the church that she had gone online to purchase a gift certificate to Red Robin for me so that I could enjoy many, many cheeseburgers. She wanted to give me the hard copy, but "just couldn't quite figure out how to make the internet work right." She went on to challenge my congregation to surround me with love for the next couple of years. "This is your chance to shine," she told them. She even told the church that it was up to them to make sure that my family and I got to Disney this year. Wow! Talk about embarrassing! She was not letting anyone off of the hook. Only Laura Early!

Again at the end of the service, Danelle and I stood by the back door and greeted people as they left. It was hard. It was hard to see people trying to hold back tears because they know that there is so much of life that you are going to miss. It is hard to know that what you said has caused so much pain. It is hard because you also know that this is just the first of many days like this when you are going to have to go through a personal trauma in a public way. It was just hard.

***

So what did this day teach me? I learned that delivering difficult news is a learned skill. It does not come naturally. There are not many people who intuitively know how to tell good people bad things. The key to giving difficult news is to be clear, be brief, and be ready to accept whatever their response is.

Be clear. This sounds obvious but it is not. So often what is clear in our minds comes out confused when we say it and leaves the recipients completely baffled. It is okay to write it down ahead of time and read it if you need to, but be clear. Even though we thought we were clear, some people still misunderstood. There was a rumor the following week that I was going to be dead in a few weeks. Now it is possible that I could get hit by a truck tomorrow, but the current prognosis is that it will not be the cancer that kills me that quickly. To this day I have no idea where they got that information, but somewhere along the line something I said was confused or misunderstood, then changed and magnified until it became catastrophic.

Be brief. Just as important as being clear is to be brief. Essentially after the initial shock of the bad news, most people simply cannot hear anymore. They completely shut down. Brevity is essential in getting the basic facts out. You can always go back and fill in the details later.

Lastly, and this is the tough part, be ready to accept their response, whatever it is. People respond to difficult news in a myriad of ways. Some shut down and won't be able to look you in the eye. Some will cling to you and cry. Some will just shake their head and shake your hand and say, "I am sorry" over and over again. It is fascinating really. When you have to tell people you have cancer, you often end up comforting them. That was another unexpected occurrence for me. It never dawned on me that I would spend so much time consoling people about my illness. It happens. People do not know what to say. It can be awkward. Let it be awkward. Your friends will deal with it in unexpected ways and that is okay. Help them deal with it. Helping them deal with it will also help you process it.

Lord of the Sabbath, forgive me for all of the times I thought myself too busy to rest in Your presence. Thank You for people who love me enough to want to die for me, who are willing to correct me in love, and ask big things of me. God, help me to rest in Your presence now and forevermore. Amen.

Chapter 8 Getting Back to "Normal"

*"How wonderful it is that nobody need wait a single
moment before starting to improve the world."*
Anne Frank, German Jewish schoolgirl

Whatever you do, do it from the heart for the Lord and not for people.
Colossians 3:23

Thank God for Thurman. Thurman texted me on Sunday
after my "summer vacation" and asked if we were meeting
Monday morning for our previously scheduled work project. I
confirmed that we were still on and would meet him at the
designated place to work.

Thurman was inviting me back to something that was
normal—work.

What we worked on is really inconsequential; what was
important is that the project we worked on during most of the
morning had nothing to do with my cancer. Oh, sure, it came up,
but Thurman is one of those friends who allows you get away with
not having to retell the entire story over again and just takes things
as they are. Mostly, we worked. We laid out schedules, made plans,
and assigned tasks. We labored for a couple of hours, and for those
hours everything was normal. Nobody was looking at me like I was

dying. Nobody asked how the rest of my family was taking "the news." It was just work—meaningful productive work—and I needed it. As a reward, we went to Five Guys for a cheeseburger (get the feeling there is a theme here?).

It is commonly understood that men, particularly, derive a great sense of their self-worth from their vocational achievement. We tie who we are to what we do. I am not saying it's right, I am just acknowledging that it *is*. That day, getting back to doing something productive helped me reclaim an important piece of my life.

I think we also forget that work is a creation of the Creator. God's first activity in the book of Genesis was an act of love and an act of labor. Work is the root word of worship (which means "work of the people"); it is what the people of God are designed and commissioned to do. I recently came to the amazing realization that retirement is not a biblical concept. Retirement is a product of the postmodern, factory-centered culture to which we have become accustomed. God gave the first woman and man significant work to do, just like God has given us significant work to do. Meaningful work creates a sense of accomplishment, provides a sense of purpose, and allows you to invest in something that will outlive you. Sure, not every task is "fun" or even meaningful, but the sum of your labor should make the world a better place and help bring some of God's kingdom into the here and now.

Meaningful work creates a sense of accomplishment. At the end of a hard day, whether it is completing something big at your job, sweating in your garden, or taking care of your children, there is a sense of accomplishment. Perhaps you assisted a coworker in being more productive or just gave them a word of encouragement. Maybe you pulled weeds all day just so your vegetables could receive more nourishment from the earth. Perhaps you helped your child take her first steps or say his first word. Either way, at the end of those days you fall exhausted into your bed and give thanks for a day where something significant was accomplished. That is a good day…no, that is a great day! I love to be exhausted from a day when the work I have undertaken has produced something. That is why at the end of every day of the creation story in the book of Genesis, when God had been up to his elbows in the dirt of creation, God closes the day with the words, "and God saw that it was good."

Meaningful work provides a sense of purpose. We all want to do something that matters. We struggle with those existential questions like, "Why am I here?" and "What difference does my life make?" Meaningful work provides a sense of purpose. Even if your job is just a job, at the end of the day it provides resources for you to support yourself and family. As a parent, I believe that our greatest purpose is to prepare the next generation to love deeply, live passionately, and listen to God intentionally. Work provides you the ability to make that happen. You provide a home, not just a house. You provide opportunities for learning, discipleship, and, as my mother would say, "good home training." Some of my most meaningful days have not been those days when I earned the most money or taught the best lesson, they have been on the days when I have tucked my child into her bed, safe and snug with a stuffed animal under her arm, and thanked God for giving me the chance to make a difference by providing a place for her. That is a sense of purpose worth working for.

Meaningful work allows you to invest in things that will outlive you. I've never seen a hearse towing a trailer. It doesn't matter how much you make, how much stuff you accumulate, how awesome your widget collection is, you can't take it with you. Every day meaningful work allows you to make an investment in relationships. You have the chance to invest in other's self-understanding and personal growth. You have the chance to invest in being joyful and sharing that joy with others. My friend Sue says there are some people who can "suck the joy out of Jesus." Do not be that person; be the person that shares the joy of Jesus. Since I've been sick I have received random notes and messages from people who have passed through my life who have thanked me for sharing love and life lessons with them. Some of them have surprised me because I did not realize I made an impact at all, but they believe that our time together changed them. Every day you have a chance to invest in the lives of others. Do not waste it!

***

My biggest fear is not death. While I have struggled to understand what God has next for me, being forever in His presence is awe-inspiring. It will be a welcomed transition from living in a world separated from God. I think my biggest fear is that I will, due to pain or medication, cease to be able to engage in meaningful work. I fear that my mind will become fuzzy from pain medication, and my ability to work will be impeded by physical limitations. That is why I have never understood "couch cruisers," people who spend all their time watching mindless television and sitting on the sofa. I appreciate those times—now more than ever—but most of the time I want to be bringing something good into the world. I want to look out my window at the end of the day and see flowers planted, or the deck completed, or I want to have a blog post published or sermon written. I want to have worked.

I know your job is tough. So is mine. But take time to cherish those days, however seldom they may come, when at the end of the day your work has provided you with a sense of accomplishment, a sense of purpose, and you have made a difference in somebody's life. Those are the things that will outlive you.

So, thank God for Thurman; and Tom who kept a previously scheduled meeting with me. Thank God for Jeff, Garry, Christine, and everybody else that week who helped me ease back into meaningful work. Thank God for people who are ready to partner with you to change the world. Thank God for work, because work is really an act of worship.

Thank You God that from the dawn of creation You chose to give Your people meaningful work. While we confess that we grumble and complain about the labors before us, we admit that we should be thankful to be able to engage in activities that provide for our families, make the world better, and help Your kingdom come on earth as it is in heaven! Amen.

Chapter 9 You've Got To Have Friends

"True friendship is a plant of slow growth and must undergo and withstand the shocks of adversity before it is entitled to the appellation."
George Washington, president

There are persons for companionship, but then there are friends who are more loyal than family. Proverbs 18:25

Nobody should have to do this alone…

While up until now most of this story has been predominately my story, there are many other stories woven into "my story." One of the things Danelle and I returned to was the fact that on Monday, when I went back to work with Thurman, Danelle (who is the director of our small, struggling, non-profit theatre company, Activate Drama) returned to face twenty-eight excited, young actors. On Monday while I was working, Danelle had to face those young people with the news that I had cancer. By now our reserves had run dry. Danelle had a camp to run, and we needed help.

Thankfully Danelle is a magnet for young adults who are anxious to learn and willing to help. She also has friends who volunteer countless hours every time we produce a show to help make it happen. During my illness I have found that there are three kinds of people. There are those who are sorry you are sick, shake their head, and move on. There are those who genuinely love you and you know that you can count on them when something comes up. Then there are people who step boldly into the moment with you and not only discover what needs to be done, they do it. They are the "ask forgiveness not permission" type folks. They are people like Bryan, who decided that not only was I not going to lead the scenery crew (usually my job during the camps), I was to stay away and recover from being in the hospital. He personally led the crew in designing, building, and tearing down the set. And they are people like Roger, who did some amazing scenery work, and Mesa who shouldered new levels of responsibility and was ready at a moment's notice for anything Danelle needed. Edward and Elaine, the power team from the local Christian school showed up just to help comfort and pray with young people who did not know how to deal with the emotions and questions that arise when somebody you know gets sick.

And there were young people who rose to new levels of commitment. Shelby, the young assistant director, took on new levels of responsibility that a year prior she would have never thought she could. Ray became Bryan's right hand and did anything that was needed without hesitation or question. And the rest of the team: Katie, Matty, David, Gracen, Chavonne, Thomas, Caleb—I do not even know them all. But I saw what it was like to have a village come along side my family and return the love that we have always tried to give them without expecting anything in return.

And then, there was Melissa. Every now and then God puts people into your path that you know are going to be with you for the rest of your life. For Danelle, Melissa is that person. They met in graduate school, were roommates for two years, and have maintained a close friendship ever since. They have been through each other's weddings, marriages, divorces, vocational challenges, and relational struggles and remained not only friends, but sisters by selection.

And like Danelle, Melissa is a theatre person. She is an amazing director, a master organizer, and the one person that can look Danelle Cauley in the face and tell her she will handle it (of course, she will have to stand on a stool because she is only 4'11").

On Tuesday evening, after driving five hours across two states, Melissa blew into town and landed at our dinner table ready to get to work the next day to get this show going. If that wasn't enough, Melissa brought her husband, Darren, a gifted musician and vocal teacher. Just about the time our frail shell of sanity was about to crack, real friends took time out of their busy lives to spend the next six days helping with the show, working (and crying) with us, and holding us together.

When Darren and Melissa arrived, Danelle began to relax. Right away our family started joking about the situation. Melissa joined right in; Darren was not able to laugh about it yet. As the meal wound down, Jacob asked to be excused and Darren joined him in the living room. This gave Melissa a chance to cry with Danelle and me. We all needed that.

As I watched Danelle absorb strength from Melissa I felt relieved that my wife would have some support. She needed it.

As we finally called it a night and settled into bed, I realized how blessed we are with friends. I was very grateful for my friends before the diagnosis, and after it, well…let's just say, praise the Lord for the people He puts in our paths to walk the journey with us.

***

There is a popular poem, author unknown, that says people come into our lives for "a reason, a season, or a lifetime." I have come to believe that God sends you who you need and sends you to where you are needed. I believe that every relationship we have is a divine gift. Even those challenging relationships have something to teach us. Who has God sent into your life to help you? Where has God sent you to be a help?

Gracious God who is always with me during the tough times in my journey, thank You God for sending those who are willing to travel with me even through dark places. I admit that some times when I need community the most, I fail to let others in. Thank You for those who barge into my life and help me when I am not even ready to ask for help. In the name of the One who comes into my troubles and carries my burden for me, Jesus, I pray. Amen.

Chapter 10 Vague Medical Language

*"If there were nothing wrong in the world,
there wouldn't be anything for us to do."*
George Bernard Shaw, dramatist, writer & critic

God isn't a God of disorder but of peace. 1 Corinthians 14:33a

So many words, so little information…

It was the week after my official diagnosis and my visit to the Duke Cancer Center before it dawned on me how little I knew about my disease and how incredibly vague all of the medical professionals had been. In our litigious culture where you can get sued for saying the wrong thing, professionals have learned the art of giving you information that is so vague that it can be interpreted in a myriad of ways.

I had a lot of questions, and nobody would give me a straight answer. Yes, I knew that my official diagnosis was neuroendocrine tumors of unknown origin in the peri-pancreatic region with metastases to the liver totaling seventeen centimeters (roughly the size of a grapefruit), but what the heck does that mean? So much comes at you so fast during the initial interactions that you hardly know what to ask. I reviewed what I did know.

One, I do not have typical (if there is such a thing)

pancreatic cancer that usually has a mortality rate of almost 100% and a survival expectancy of only a few months. Neuroendocrine cancer grows much more slowly than other cancers, but how slow? I had no idea. Dr. Hope explained that we had come into the story of my cancer in the middle of the narrative. She went on to say that while we could see what had developed in the past, we had no idea how long it had been growing, how long it took to metastasize, or how fast it was spreading. We would need more tests over more time to gain that understanding. Lots of explanation without much clarity.

Two, I had "many, many months." When you go from having three to six months to "many, many," you do not really think to ask how many that really is. Was it six hundred, sixty, or sixteen? When you have cancer, you live in a sort of time-lapse ambiguity. There is a time bomb in your body that is ticking at its own, individual rate and you do not get the luxury of a clock on the outside to let you know when it is going to explode. Because of the many variables, getting a doctor to give you an estimate of life expectancy is akin to getting the president's nuclear codes. So, what do you do? You go online and research articles about your disease to get a better understanding of your prognosis (which is probably a bad idea). The only problem is that even those studies are simultaneously fact filled and incredibly vague.

Three, the kind of cancer I have is considered "rare." Not only is it rare, it is usually asymptomatic (fancy word for not having any symptoms until it is too late) until it is in the later stages and is usually misdiagnosed as irritable bowel syndrome (IBS) or acid reflux (which I've had since grad school). In most cases the patient has the symptoms for many years until they become so severe that the doctor runs the right test or orders the right scan and they realize something more serious is happening. Like in my case it is usually discovered by accident and not until it has metastasized and there is extensive distant organ involvement (sometimes referred to as "late stage" or "stage IV").

My sister-in-law, Jaimie, is convinced that my rough and tumble ride on the roller coaster impacted the site of my cancer causing it to spasm, thus allowing for its discovery. Otherwise, I would still be living my normal, everyday, "I am gonna live till I am 90" life.

Now for the things I do not know. First, I have no idea "how" I will be living. Will things go along as they had been? Will I continue to be asymptomatic, or will I be one of those cancer patients wracked with pain? Will I be able to keep working? You see, for me it was not just about how long I will be alive, but *how* I will be alive. I want to live every minute I have left. I am determined that I will not "be" the cancer. I will live "with" the cancer. The cancer will not define me. Coincidentally, it was about this time that my friend Draughon contacted me. He said he had a gift for me. The gift was a stack of t-shirts that said, "I am Not Dead Yet!" (Thank you Monty Python!) This is when I came up with my life theme that I have already mentioned a few times: to love deeply, live passionately, and listen to God intentionally.

Secondly, I do not know how I will handle living while knowing I am dying. When you have cancer, it is always there in the back of your mind. Things take on greater significance. Little things you take for granted like dinner with your family, the embrace of a friend, and laughter seem to have bigger meaning than you ever realized. How was I going to handle my mortality? I have known so many people who have just given up and given in to dying. They received a difficult diagnosis or had a life trauma and then just curled up and ceased to live long before they actually died. They may have lived for years longer, but something died on the inside. I did not want to be one of the walking dead, a cancer zombie.

Next, I do not know how long I have left to live. The real quandry is that I am not sure I want to know. The "unknowing" forces me to be more proactive. It allows me to say "no" to things that I do not have the energy to invest in and "yes" to the things that support my new life's theme. It is as though I can hear the clock ticking but I cannot see the time. I am fully aware of the brevity of my life but not sure when time will be up. This ambiguity is both empowering and incredibly frustrating.

Lastly, and perhaps the most disturbing piece of the puzzle that is missing, is how will I die? Neuroendocrine tumors are usually not the cause of death, they are the catalyst for other things to happen. They cause organ failure or fatal digestive issues. There are complications like lung and heart issues or eventual liver failure. There are so many options, and none of them are good.

***

So how do I handle not knowing how long I will live, how I am going to live, or how I am going to handle the lingering knowledge of my eminent demise? I decided to handle these challenges one moment at a time. Yes, the ambiguity of not having a date on my calendar to plan my funeral is extremely frustrating. It would be so much easier if cancer just came with an expiration date. Then you would know whether to plan that trip to England or not (I now buy travel insurance, just in case). How do I handle not knowing "how" I am going to live? I just live, this moment; it is the only one I have anyway. I seize the moments when I feel good, when I am able to be productive and I suck the life out of them so that when I have to stop in the middle of the afternoon just to rest, it is okay. I am just learning to live in the "now" and quit worrying about the "what's next." How do I handle knowing I am going to die? Well, I have always known I was going to die, I just thought there was more sand in the hourglass. Yes, the sadness creeps in around the edges when I think of all the things I will miss, but that makes me want to live a little more passionately right now. I refuse to die before I am dead. I know the clock is ticking and ticking loudly. That just makes me want to make every moment one to be remembered.

I tell my congregation all the time, "I do not know what

tomorrow holds, but I know Who holds tomorrow." At the risk of packing too many clichés into one paragraph, I also remind them that "yesterday is gone, tomorrow will never get here, all you have is now; that is why it is called the present." Yes I am dying and it sucks, but right now I am living, and as long as I am living then I am going to live it up!

Gracious God, who holds tomorrow, help me live for You today, and live every day to the fullest. In the name of the One who redeems my past, restores my hope in the present, and who holds my future, Jesus, I pray. Amen

Chapter 11 Nap Time

"A peace above all earthly dignities, a still and quiet conscience."
William Shakespeare, playwright & poet

God lets me rest in grassy meadows; He leads me to restful waters.
Psalm 23:2

It was good to go back to being productive on the Monday
following my diagnosis. I needed to go back to work to regain some
sense of normalcy. In hindsight, I should have taken more time to
slowly reenter the world. As the commercial says, "Life comes at
you fast." Jumping back in to a nearly full schedule five days after I
was diagnosed with terminal cancer was too fast.

Thinking back, I realize that I should have returned to
work much more slowly. Rather than keep the grueling schedule
that I had arranged before I was sick, I should have eased back into
my vocational duties. I think I was trying to prove to myself that I
was still in the game. Nobody would have questioned my need to
reschedule a meeting or lighten my load, but I was in a state
between denial and determination. I was going to prove to myself
that this thing, this "Damn Cancer" (damn cancer usually
abbreviated DC around my house…sorry friends who do not like
swear words, but it is what I call it) was not going to be my boss. It

was not going to limit me. It was not going to slow me down. I was going to press through and press on. I had overcome being raised in a broken home, living in a low-income family, academic struggles, and cultural challenges. This would not be the thing that broke me. Like so many times in my life, I had something to prove.

I was trying to prove to myself, and to everyone around me, that I was still able to work. I wanted to prove that I still have value. I was trying to prove to others that I was still productive. I was trying to prove that I was still alive. I was trying to validate my identity.

But every afternoon somewhere between 3:00 and 4:00 pm I ran out of steam. Oh, I usually started the day strong. I launched into my day...okay, I eased into my day after a couple of cups of coffee, but that is the way it had always been. I eased into my day and made every effort to keep a full schedule. The problem is that in the middle of the afternoon my body would involuntarily slow down. If I did not stop and rest for an hour or so, I would be essentially useless (and I am told, very grumpy) the rest of the evening. Something was going to have to change, and that was going to be the expectation I was placing on myself.

My identity could no longer be proven by how much I accomplished in a day. My identity was going to have to be validated, not by my own accomplishments, but by what Christ was working within me. It is amazing how much God speaks when you have to stop and listen. I believe that too often we do not hear God because we fail to actually stop and listen. Suddenly, I was forced to take time in the middle of every afternoon to quit doing and just "be." Yes, more often than not this involves a nap, and it also involves time when I do not have the ability to generate content or even compose a cohesive thought; but I do have the ability to be in God's presence and listen for the voice of God's Son.

***

There are stages in every mature relationship. In the beginning, you talk continuously. You are anxious for the other person to know you and to get to know them. Later, you grow closer and, while communication is still essential, there is space for quiet in the midst of life's noise. In some mature relationships, I have seen couples who are just content to be in each other's presence, perhaps holding hands. They can sit still and quietly enjoy being near the one they love. That is what this time in the afternoon became for me, a time to just sit in God's presence and be with Christ. It was not a time for a litany of lists or any pre-formulated prayers. It was just a time to be with God, not asking for anything, not complaining about anything, not even confessing anything; just being. This ancient practice is called "centering prayer" because it reminds you of Who should be at the center of your life.

How ironic that it took terminal illness for me to slow down consistently and listen to God. I have tried on many occasions to get into the habit of centering prayer, of spending regular, unscripted time with the Creator of the universe, but the world kept creeping in. The schedule kept filling up. The time kept ebbing away, and the best-laid plans for focused spiritual solitude gave away to the desire to be productive. Now, my ability to be productive is almost solely dependent upon my taking the time to rest. Now my identity can no longer be based upon my accomplishments and abilities. It is found in my being in relationship with Christ. I have become more of a human being than just a human doing.

I realized this about Wednesday and that was the day I decided to ask for the impossible…

Gracious God help me to just spend time in Your presence, not asking for anything, not needing anything except to be with You and to be in Your presence. Thank You God that Your Son has made it possible for us to simply be with You. Amen.

Chapter 12 Recovery Leave

*"Thou hast made us for thyself, O Lord, and our heart
is restless until it finds its rest in thee."*
Augustine of Hippo, Confessions

I say to myself, I wish I had wings like a dove! I'd fly away and rest.
Psalm 55:6

Living with open hands.

Like I said, on Wednesday I decided to ask for a miracle. I needed a break. I needed to get away.

By Wednesday I realized two things. First, I realized that my vacation had not been a vacation; it had been emergency medical leave with a side order of trauma and some gut wrenching, life altering news to boot. Secondly, I came to the realization that I was spiritually, emotionally, and physically exhausted. Danelle is always kidding me about networking. I have friends and acquaintances all over the place and use social media to manage all of them. I use my networks and social media to spread the word about the great things I find. She jokingly said that I should get online and use all those contacts and see if anyone would let me use a place at the beach for a week to recover after our drama camps were finished and before everyone had to return to school.

So I did. I put on my Facebook status a link to my blog, *"My Summer Vacation,"* and asked if anyone knew anybody with a condo or beach place that my family could use for a week to recover from the devastating news of my illness and spend some time together trying to figure out how to make the most out of the life we had left. I did it, hoping for a couple of days at somebody's timeshare. What I got was a blessing well beyond my expectation.

That very afternoon, I received a private message from an acquaintance, literally a friend of a friend, who had a friend at a real estate company on the Outer Banks of North Carolina. Did you get that? This was not somebody who knew my family or me. This was a friend two or three times removed. They had nothing to gain. There was no incentive or motivation for them to help me. This amazing woman at the real estate company had taken it upon herself to contact some of their homeowners who had vacant homes for the week we wanted to be away and found one to donate. The owner gave the realtor permission for us to use a three-bedroom home just seventy yards from the ocean. This home normally rents for more than $2,500 per week, and there was no way we could afford such a place. By Thursday afternoon I was returning the paperwork to secure the house for a week of recovery leave.

Why would anybody do this for us? I was blown away. I had not been to the beach for a full week since I was seventeen. Now I was going to be able to spend time on the edge of the land looking out the front door into the rolling waves and early morning sunrises over the crystal coast of North Carolina.

Danelle and I have always tried to live our lives with open hearts, open hands, and an open home. We have fed hundreds of people gathered around our dinner table (not all at the same time). We have invited struggling college students and families with children to live with us for a while until they could get back on their feet. We sponsor *Compassion International* children, give gifts to orphans in Africa through ZOE Ministry rather than exchange

Christmas gifts, and try to model a life of faithful stewardship for our children. We are people who love to give. There is something I've noticed about people who like to give; we are not very good at receiving.

Now we are receiving. It is rather humbling, actually. This gift was so overwhelming it brought tears to our eyes. It was truly an act of grace, an act of undeserved, unmerited, and extravagant generosity. The amazing thing is, this was just the first of the gifts we have been offered. Other people have come forward with offers to use their vacation homes when we need to get away for a time of solitude and respite. My congregation has accepted Dr. Laura Early's challenge to help me spend a week at Walt Disney World with my family. After putting on my "bucket list" that I have always wanted to visit England, I was contacted by *Alpha Tours* and was offered the opportunity for Danelle and I to visit the United Kingdom and tour historical Methodist sites. Meals have been dropped off and love given in such abundance that it is sometimes hard to understand. There are some days I can hardly believe the blessings people are heaping upon us.

I had breakfast with my best friend, David, shortly after these things started happening. I explained that I could not understand why people were being so generous. We had not done anything to deserve these gifts. David just shook his head and said, "What would you do if it was somebody you knew? You would do everything in your power to give them whatever you could. People see that in you and want to give back to you for all the things you have given to others throughout your ministry." I just sat there, stunned, because I had never given a thought to what Danelle and I have given away. We had always just tried to listen to God's direction and then do what He said. We are not ones to count the cost, because what we have received from God is so much more than we could ever give.

***

When God sent his Son, God gave us the greatest gift ever given. God gave us the gift of life, and it was a gift of great love. *"For God so loved the world that He gave his only Son, that whoever believes in Him might have eternal life."* (John 3:16, CEB) God loved, so God gave. If we really love God then we are, by the very nature of being loved, givers of anything we have. When I die I will not be taking anything with me. Nothing I own is ever really mine forever; it is only mine for a short time. It is going to pass through my hands. Sometimes God gives me the chance to let it go now so I can bless others. That is awesome. I get to do, in some small way, what God did. I get to show love by being a giver and not a grasper.

I know people who are graspers. They hold onto everything as tightly as they can, unwilling to let anything go. They do it with stuff. They do it with relationships. They do it with their time. The ironic thing is that they cannot receive the blessings God has for them with full hands.

One of the practices I teach my congregation is a prayer position with both hands up, open, and empty. One hand reminds us that there is nothing we have that God did not give us. The other reminds us that we are ready to receive whatever God has for us. Together, they are open, to remind us to keep our hearts, hands, and homes open to do whatever God calls us to do. Pray that way some time. You will find your prayer takes on a whole new feeling. Rather than going to God with a list, go to God and ask what is it you have that you need to let go of, and what is it that God has that you need to receive.

I am learning to receive. The Scripture reminds us that God has given *"far beyond all that we could ask or imagine"* (Ephesians 3:20, CEB). What I am learning is that when you receive what somebody else wants to give, you allow God to bless *them* in a completely new way. I would never want to be the reason that somebody else was not blessed. So I am learning to receive. Plus, what is the use in asking for a miracle if you are not willing to accept it when it comes?

Gracious God who gives more than I can ask or imagine, I come to You with my hands up, open, and empty. I remember that there is nothing I have that You did not give me. I am open to whatever you would have me to receive. I desire to open my heart, my hands, and my home for You to use to bring Your kingdom come on earth as it is in heaven. Help me to give as You gave; to receive whatever You would have me to receive. In the One who gave everything, Jesus, so that I could receive eternal life I pray. Amen.

Chapter 13 You Have a Cancer Too
The message I shared the first Sunday after my diagnosis.

*"We do not need magic to transform our world.
We carry all of the power we need inside ourselves already."*
J.K. Rowling, author

"Therefore, I urge you, brothers, in view of God's mercy, to offer your bodies as living sacrifices, holy and pleasing to God—this is your spiritual act of worship. Do not **conform** *any longer to the pattern of this world, but be* **transformed** *by the renewing of your mind. Then you will be able to test and approve what God's will is—his good, pleasing and perfect will."*
Romans 12:1-2

A Note About this Chapter

This chapter is a little different than the ones before it or after it. It is essentially the manuscript for a message I shared with the congregation I was serving during the time of my initial diagnosis. Because it is meant to be delivered orally, it is in the second person, rather than the first person. I included it because I think this message includes some of my key learnings and clarifies some things that are otherwise unclear. Almost everyone struggles with why "bad things happen to good people." My congregation was really having a difficult time with my illness (just like I was).

This is part of my discovery process.

I love PlayDoh® . Every time I smell it, I am a little kid again with purple clay under my nails. I love the feel of it squeezing between my fingers. You know what I love most? With PlayDoh and a little imagination you can make anything. Now some of us can only make snakes and hotdogs. Some can sculpt more elaborate things. Some kids get all the accessories and special shaping tools. All I ever had was a plastic knife and plenty of time, but still, with this brightly colored children's modeling clay and a little creativity, you can create your own world. We were made to create, you and I.

In Romans 12, Paul reminds us of several things in these short verses. He challenges us to allow ourselves to be PlayDoh® in the hands of God; to let God unleash the amazing and creative power that is within us, often trapped by our own self-perceived and self-inflicted limitations. Paul is pushing us not to be formed, or rather conformed, to the mold that the world traps us in. We are people with the ability to be *transformed*, made completely new. When we let God in and allow that to happen, we will fully embrace who God is. Suddenly the presence of the divine Creator is revealed in the life of the fallen creation. The image of God shines through more fully when embraced completely.

We are FORMED.

I am sure sometimes you may get tired of me reminding you that you were formed in the image of God. In Genesis 1:27, the Bible explains that God, in God's infinite wisdom and power, got elbow deep into our lives and formed us personally from the dust of the earth. You and I (and all of humanity) were formed in God's image; we have within us the "imago Dei," God's own image.

Sometimes that image is hard to see. It is hard to look in the mirror when you see the bags under your eyes, the struggles of life written on your face, and see God in there trying to release God's creative power in your life. But God is there. Maybe He is buried deep beneath the hurt and pain, covered by the dust of long forgotten dreams and a worry-laden soul.

Psalm 139 says you were knit together by God's own hands while inside your mom. WOW! Think about that for a moment. It is simply incredible that two random cells ran into each other and there you were, an egg and a single sperm cell united and at that moment your life began. Two cells became four, four became eight, eight became sixteen, and eventually your heart started beating independently of your mother's. You attached yourself to your mom and she started feeding you and you grew. Fingers and toes were molded by the hand of God, eyes and eyelashes were shaped. Even that freckle on your shoulder or that birthmark you wish you did not have was carefully sculpted by the hands of the Master, making you to be you, uniquely formed with a plan, path, and purpose for your life. Then you started kicking and rolling and keeping your mom up at night (you'd be doing this for a few years).

One day, on your appointed day, the day that the Scripture says was written in "the Book," you had a big coming out party. You entered the world in the midst of a difficult process. You went from the safety of the womb to the harshness the hospital room. Your public life began, like everyone's life begins, under pressure. The pressure of life continues for the rest of your days. Once you entered the room, you did what the rest of us wish we could do when we face the cold, cruel world—you screamed for all you were worth, and God was there.

One of the amazing things about your creation is that those cells created you from the inside out. Isn't that awesome? The inside formed the outside. Go online and watch one of those videos that show you the progression of a child growing through time lapsed photography inside its mother's womb. Isn't that cool? The stuff on the inside shaped the stuff on the outside. Just like the way your soul shapes the rest of your life. The inside molds the outside.

A famous sculptor was once asked how he could turn a slab of rock into a beautiful statue, he replied, "I just release what's on the inside." God formed you from the inside, but if we are not careful we let the outside hold the inside back.

The other amazing thing to realize once you understand that you are molded from the inside out is that no matter what, even if you were a "divine surprise" like me, you are a creation of God. Even your flaws flowed from the hand of God. It is our differences that make us interesting. It is the variant brush strokes that make a painting a masterpiece. It is the lines on our faces that make us unique and tell the stories of our lives. As part of the creation story, God is continuously trying to help you unleash the beauty within you. Do you know why you have such a tough time letting it out? You struggle to unleash that beauty because the world seeks to conform us to its image and that actually deforms and mal-forms us.

We have been De-formed and Mal-formed by the sin in the world.

The world seeks to conform you to its understanding of "beauty." To its flawed understanding of "success." To its corrupted understanding of happiness and contentment. Unfortunately, those messages so saturate our lives that before long, when we look into the mirror, all we see is what is wrong, and we push the *imago Dei* (image of God) farther and farther into the background. We start to measure the outside, forgetting that God's presence is formed from the inside.

You are exposed to as many as 3,000 advertising messages a day, that is more than 20,000 every week. Every one of those messages is trying to tell you that if you buy what they are peddling, your life will be better. You will be more conformed to the image of beauty, success, or happiness they have set for you.

You are exposed to more advertising messages in a week than previous generations were in their entire lifetime. Billboards and signs line our roads; banners surround our email; and I bet when you check your mail there are at least two flyers, postcards, or advertisement letters waiting to tell you how you can live better in exchange for a few of your hard-earned dollars. The world is awfully good at pushing you to conform.

When I was working my way through college, I used to substitute teach to make extra money. I worked with all ages from kindergarten to high school, depending on who needed me that day. I began to notice something a bit distressing. In kindergarten you could dump a pile of broken crayons in the middle of the table, pass out recycled paper, and ask who could draw a picture for you. Hands would fly into the air. They would attack the work with the intensity only possessed by a determined five year old. They would cover the entire page with color and figures. When you asked them to hold up their drawings, with great pride they would explain their illustrations. It did not matter if you could understand it; they knew exactly what they had drawn and could see it clearly and share it passionately.

Take that same class and fast-forward to sixth or seventh grade, provide them with sharpened, colored pencils and drawing paper and ask them who can draw. Out of thirty students you might have one or two who offer up that they can draw specific things, maybe a horse, or an anime character. They resist exposing their limited artistic abilities and certainly would not want to stand in front of their peers and share their creations. What happened? What killed the creative impulse burning within them at five but is all but gone at thirteen?

Criticism. When you were young you memorized a rhyme that went something like this, "Sticks and stones may break my bones, but words will never hurt me." That is a lie, by the way. The emotional and spiritual pain of negative words stings far worse and for far longer than any physical assault. Your peers' scathing words telling you that you are not good enough and how much you "suck." Those words sting your soul, crush your creative impulse, and cover up that divine light of creativity God placed within you.

A recent survey revealed that we tend to receive five times more negative feedback than positive. For every word of affirmation, you receive five times more criticism, sarcastic and hurtful words, or just plain insults. No wonder the power of hope is so dim in our lives. It is easier to find a problem than a solution. We are obsessed with what is wrong, imperfect, or flawed about who we are. We so want to "conform to the pattern of this world" that we forget that we are formed in the *imago Dei*. It is a heart issue.

What is your heart seeking? Are you trying to become the artificial image the world is advertising, or are you seeking to release the image of God that is in you?

Cancer is when some cells, once perfectly healthy, mutate and begin to become something that is damaging to the larger system. It starts out small. Just a cell or two of malignancy, then it spreads. Soon it makes the jump to other parts of your body; that's called metastasis. Left unchecked, it will run rampant through your organs and bones and kill you from the inside out. When you let the world conform you, you fuel a cancer in your soul. You allow something that you have hidden within you to begin to kill you.

You have cancer. It might not be like mine. I have neuroendocrine tumors. This form of cancer is slowly spreading. By the time we caught it, it had already metastasized to my liver. The treatment I am receiving is designed to slow the growth, but currently there is no cure. Save for the miraculous hand of God (which I still believe is possible), it will be this or complications caused by this disease that eventually kills me. I have cancer, but you have a cancer too.

Your cancer might not be the physical kind that has invaded my body. But it could be some past pain, some unresolved hurt, some unreconciled relationship that is eating you alive from the inside. Something is eating you emotionally. Something is keeping you from growing your relationship with others. It could be guilt over the past, pain in the present, or worry over the future. Something is eating you spiritually, keeping you from deepening your relationship with God. The world surrounds us with negativity, hate, and criticism that burn a hole in our soul and plants seeds of destruction within us. Those cancerous cells take hold and begin to grow, then spread, and if you are not careful they consume you and kill you from the inside out. But there is hope.

What You Need is Transformation

We have been formed, and the world has done its best to deform and mal-form us, but deep within your heart you crave to be reformed. The problem is that despite what the best self-help book says, we cannot do it ourselves. What we really need is to be transformed from the inside out by the same hands that formed us.

Drop by the local bookstore and you will see shelves heavy with books and magazines telling you that you can change yourself. They promote the world's unrealistic standards of perfection. Almost every day syndicated media "doctors" and self-help "experts" make big money yelling at people to re-form themselves. They challenge viewers and listeners to make different choices and change their behaviors. What do these and the hundreds of other gurus and infomercial or YouTube experts have in common? They are telling you how to change the outside but forgetting the inside. There is the presupposition that if you impose the change from the outside, it will bring the inside into alignment.

There is something you need to know, and it goes against all the self-help books and articles you've been reading…ready? YOU CAN'T DO IT! Sometimes you can behave your way into a new way of being, but the motivation and inspiration has to begin on the inside, at a soul and cellular level. Paul made it clear when he was writing his letter to the church in Rome because they kept getting the inside and the outside mixed up. People thought that faith was about how they acted on the outside, the kind of friends they had, and the kind of clothes they wore. They were trying to impress each other. Outward appearance was everything. Perception was more important than character. Does that sound familiar? The problem is that this creates a shallow façade and when difficulty arises, the façade crumbles and you are left with an empty shell where your soul should be.

When Paul wrote about being conformed, the word he used was "schema" which is the outside shape. Remember the PlayDoh® and how you can make the image of anything you want? You can shape a bowl out of it, but if you fill that bowl with water it will eventually all run out. Why? I mean it looks like a bowl, it has the "schema" or outside form of a bowl, but it is not a bowl, is it? It is the form, but cannot perform the function.

Now go into your cabinet and get out a pottery bowl. Fill it with water. How does it hold up? What is the difference? The difference is that this bowl has been transformed. That is the image Paul gives us when he says "be transformed." The word he uses is *metamorphia*, which is an inside change. Does it sound familiar? It should, it is the root word of metamorphosis. Complete change.

What's the difference between the PlayDoh® bowl and the pottery one? Well, there are a lot of differences. There is a difference in the quality of clay, the glaze that is applied to the outside, and the formation of its shape by the skilled hands of a potter. But the biggest difference is that the clay bowl has been through the fire. The fire is what changed it from form to function. It changed the clay at a molecular level and it caused the temporary shape of the clay to become the permanent shape of the pottery. When you hear the word, metamorphosis, I bet you think of all those science class videos of butterflies changing from larva to the beautiful, flittering creatures that so often represent new life. God desires to transform your life, to create something new within you.

***

We hate difficulty, trouble, and trial, but God can use those fires in our lives to perfect us and transform us into being a usable vessel for His will, to do His work. In order to have the image of God released in your life, you must be willing to go through the transformation process. You must be willing to let God use every part of you — every experience, every pain, and every difficulty — to bring you into deeper relationship with Christ. Then you will be "transformed by the renewing of your mind." You will be changed from the inside. When your inside changes, the outside will follow. **We have to be transformed by having Christ formed within us.**

When you invite Jesus into your life to be your Savior and your Lord, you are asking God to begin a radical reworking and reshaping of who you are from the inside out. Sometimes that means you have to go through the fire. Sometimes that means you have to embrace the pain that you sought to hide, or take steps to reconcile a relationship you have struggled with. You have to invite Christ in to begin the work IN you, not TO you…get that? The work is done from the inside out.

God my Creator who has known me since I was within my mother's womb, come into my life anew today and transform me from the inside out. Jesus who gave everything that I might be made new, become Lord of my life and let me embrace the difficult times, struggles, and pain and allow them to transform me to become a vessel that can be used for your glory. In the name of the One who died to give me life, who gave everything to transform me, Jesus, I pray. Amen.

Chapter 14 Injected and Inspected

"Everything that is done in the world is done by hope."
Martin Luther, religious reformer

Lord, you have examined me. You know me. Psalm 139:1

I do not know if you have ever spent three hours in a cool room with your feet strapped together, your hands over your head, and radioactive die coursing through your veins while a rather intimidating looking machine takes 360 degree pictures of your interior, but it is not something I would recommend for your next party. Every kind of cancer requires some level of CT, SPECT, MRI, or some other type of scan, x-ray, or test to assist in the visualization and measurement of tumors. By the time I arrived at Duke for my Octreotide scan, I had already been through several sonograms and CT scans, as well as a biopsy that involved a very long needle and the proverbial "this will only hurt a little" lie. Those were just a warm up for the fun that was still to be had.

To be honest, the scan was not that bad. I am not claustrophobic — well, not much. I have some basic skills in centering prayer that helped me relax so that I could mentally and spiritually escape from the space for part of the time. The staff was very professional and efficient. I was allowed to listen to my IPOD for the longer stretches when I was to remain as immobile as possible and tried to breathe "normally." Funny thing about breathing, you do it all the time but as soon as somebody tells you to just "breathe normally," you automatically become hyper-conscious of your breathing and begin panting like a dog on a hot day. Even now that I have mentioned it you are more aware of your breathing, just like reading the word "YAWN" makes you want to yawn.

The Octreotide scan is designed to highlight the places in your body where the neuroendocrine cancer has metastasized, allowing the course of treatment to be adjusted accordingly. The drug they put into your veins on day one works its way through your body. On day two when you go back for the longer, more intense scan, it has attached to your tumors, along with radioactive tags. Your prayer is that the cancer is not anywhere that has not been discovered yet, like your bones or your lungs.

The good news is that you have plenty of time to pray while you are lying on your back in the machine for three hours. The bad news is that you know the technician will have the information almost immediately, but they cannot tell you anything. You have to wait for your consultation with the oncologist, or the radiologist, or whatever specialist is going to interpret the shadows and images for you. You will not know until a week later when you return for your follow up visit. By then, everybody on your medical team knows what you wish you knew, but do not really want to know. You know?

So you lie there relatively comfortably, but a little stiff; for the first time since your diagnosis you have nothing to do but think and pray. There is a certain luxury to having three uninterrupted hours inside your head. You have time to tease out a hundred different scenarios, add a few more items to your bucket list, and wonder how many mortgage payments this test is costing you. Meanwhile, the machine quietly does its job, taking nuclear pictures of your interior, documenting every organ, and highlighting those places that are "lit up" by the radioactive tags.

Then you are finished. Rather unceremoniously, the technician tells you that she has everything she needs, and you can get dressed and go home. The doctor will see you next week to discuss the results. It is amazing how far away "next week" can seem when you know that the crucial information is already on your oncologist's computer. She and the attending radiologist will have narrated the report in typical vague medical language before the end of the day and the finished diagnosis will have been determined. But you, the person who they are objectively diagnosing, the subject of the myriad of tests you are enduring, will not get to know until "next week."

Did you ever notice when you were a kid how the closer it got to your birthday, or Christmas, or summer break, the slower the days seemed to progress? As the presents piled up under the tree, the longer the days seemed to take. The anticipation caused those days to drag by. You thought Christmas would never get here. That is the way it is when you have had test after test after test. Then you have to wait until somebody reads the test, and somebody else verifies the previous reading. Yet another somebody has to check that it has been read and verified and forwarded to your doctor so that she can read what has already been read. Finally she confirms the already-verified diagnosis. Meanwhile, you are sitting on pins and needles waiting to see if there are fewer grains of sand in your hourglass than there were yesterday, not that they would actually ever tell you that. You have been injected and inspected and now you wait.

I left the second day, after spending hours on my back while hundreds of pictures were taken of my insides, and went to lunch with my friends, Jeff and Monica. When we sat down, I was a bit surprised that their two elementary-aged twins insisted on sitting on either side of me. They were so excited to see me. There is nothing to remind you of the joy of life like kids. Suddenly, a simple lunch with friends became an adventure. They, too, inspected me. Skylar, one of the twins, kept looking at me. She said, "Pastor Marty, you do not look sick." I laughed.

"That's true, I do not look sick, and most days I do not even feel sick, but inside of me there is something that is making me sick," I told her.

"Well I am just going to keep asking Jesus to take it out then," she said, and went back to coloring the picture on the placemat.

"I am going to keep asking that too, Skylar." I said.

Amazing what the faith of a child can do to give a grown man, a pastor no less, a big dose of hope. Jesus was pretty clear that we needed the "faith of a child" to see the "kingdom of God." I saw it that day, in the eyes of a little girl eating chicken strips and ice cream.

There are many ways to be injected and inspected. In the same week I was injected with radioactive medicine and scanned from head to toe, I was also injected with a big dose of hope after being inspected by a six-year-old with more faith than I have probably ever had. For Skylar, it is a foregone conclusion that Jesus is going to take care of this thing for her friend. She is asking God for big things, expecting God to handle it. She exudes hope; she gives hope.

***

When was the last time you instilled that much hope into somebody's life? Hope is free. It is so easily given with a soft word, a simple prayer, or a smile. Hope is something that we crave and something that is in incredibly short supply. We have become "hopeless" because our world is so attracted to bad news that we forget that God is doing great things around us. These great things can begin with the simplest steps of shining the light of hope into somebody's dark day.

If you have ever been camping miles away from the

artificial lights of a city you soon realize that a single candle can be seen for miles on a dark night. That is what Skylar did for me that day. She lit a candle. She ignited the candle of hope that would light my path on that day. There have been many others who have come along in the past few weeks to share a little hope, to shine a little light, and to help me find my path back to the One who promises to be the light unto my path. Thank God for those who hold the candle of hope when mine has gone out.

Jesus You promised to be a lamp unto my feet and a light unto my path. I am trusting You today for the next step. Thank You for those You place in my path who bear the light when I feel like my light is gone. Thank You for those who have boundless hope when my hope has faded. Thank You for the faith of a child that teaches me to believe again. In the name of the One who died to give me hope I pray. Amen.

Chapter 15 The Gift of Dying Slowly

"Never give in! Never give in! Never, never, never,
never—in nothing great or small, large or petty—never
give in except to convictions of honor and good sense."
Winston Churchill, British statesman

You need to persevere so that when you have done the will of God, you will
receive what he has promised. Hebrews 10:36

Today I watched my one-year-old grandson eat lunch. I am
not sure whether he got more food on him or in him. He had
yogurt spread all over his face; his hands were covered with the
remnants of everything else he was served; and drool running
down his face as he gnawed on the baby spoon he had been using
more as an instrument of destruction than as an eating utensil. It
was delightful. As I sat there and watched him eat, I thought what
a gift it is to be dying slowly.

Let us review, I have neuroendocrine tumors. What I
eventually learned is that they originated between the stomach and
the small intestine. As previously mentioned, these are slow
growing but terminal tumors. It is a relatively rare disease affecting
a comparatively small number of people each year. You might
know about this type of cancer because it is the kind that took the

lives of Dave Thomas, founder of Wendy's restaurants, and Steve Jobs, founder of Apple Computers. My doctors do not really know how long my metastasized tumors have been growing, but they think for a few years at least. They also do not know how fast they are growing and can only guess at how long I have left. With treatment, I hope to be able to remain active and working for a few more years before my life becomes more severely limited, but I am okay with that because I think it is a gift to die slowly.

So many times I have seen situations where someone dies suddenly and the ripping of that precious life from their family and friends tears the seams of their souls. Things are left unsaid. Relationships are never mended. Scars grow deeper with grief. Dying suddenly is traumatic, devastating, and leaves in its wake so many things left undone.

Dying slowly, on the other hand, provides me with the gift of time. Oh, it is not much time, but I think it might be just enough time. It reminds me to focus, with intention and passion, on the things that really matter, like watching small children smear dinner in their hair. It makes me seek out opportunities to tell stories, laugh at the past and the present. It calls me to reevaluate my life's goals and objectives. It helps me be more demonstrative with my affection toward those I care about most. Dying slowly is a gift because it reminds me that I have time to laugh, time to live, and time to love.

I have time to laugh. I love to laugh, and I have a big laugh. If you hear me laughing, you know it is me. I love to sit around a loaded dinner table and hear stories of people's lives and discover what formed them and transformed them. I love to hear stories of their disastrous first dates, and stories of their first real love. I like to tell stories, sometimes enhanced for the benefit of the listener, and hear others laugh. Dying slowly has given me the gift of making sure that I have time to laugh.

One of my daughter's friends, who is much loved by our family, talked about what it was like to have dinner with us after my diagnosis. Kasey said the way we made sarcastic jokes about cancer and dying was a little awkward at first, but soon she realized that she could jump right in and laugh with us. I have learned that if you laugh at something, you take away its power to overwhelm you. Maybe that is why I laugh at life so often — so it does not overwhelm me. I know that is why I laugh at death and cancer so often; I refuse to give in to the dark shadows that linger on the edges and try to steal my joy. I pray that I laugh until the day I die. I am going to laugh as much as I can until I am laughing in the presence of Jesus. I want to laugh as much as I can, as long as I can. Do you?

Dying slowly is a gift because it reminds me that I still have time to live. We get so busy living that we forget we are all dying. Some of us are just dying more quickly than others. We forget to go on vacation, or to enjoy the moment, or to just have ice cream. One of the amazing things that happened since I have discovered that I am dying is that I have become even more passionate about living. I think my passion for life has inspired some others to help me live as passionately as I can for as long as I can. I have had people I do not know send me gifts and offer me opportunities to check some things off my bucket list that would have never occurred had I not been dying. You know what? I am actually going to receive those gifts with thanksgiving. Gifts I would have never accepted before because as somebody who has tried to live his whole life with an open heart, open hands, and an open home I know what a blessing it is to bless others. In my life, my biggest blessings have come from what I have given away, not what I have received, so I want others to have that kind of life blessing as well! I have some time to live and I want to live it up for as much time as I have left. Do you?

Dying slowly is a gift because it reminds me that I still have time to love. I have taken to reminding everyone I encounter to "love deeply." If anything, this whole dying thing has caused me to be more open with my expressions of affection with people I might otherwise have never told. I am a man, you know, and we are not all that good at expressing affection. What the heck, I am dying. So I tell my "dude" friends that I love them because I want them to know that they are special to me. I tell my kids I love them. I tell my wife a hundred times a day that I love her, because it seems to me that I need to give out about forty years of love in about four or five years. I want the people around me to feel my love for them in whole new ways. I want to live with arms wide open and share my heart with as many people as I can. You see, I can love because I have been loved. I am loved by friends and family. I am loved so much by my wife that it seems some days I can barely contain it, more than I deserve. My greatest desire is to return that love. After all, a Savior whose stripes and scars made a way for my healing loves me. That love allows me to be freed from my own sin, situations, and scars and to show love to others like God showed love to me.

***

Dying slowly is a gift. My gift might be opened sooner than yours but I want to remind you of something: you are dying slowly as well. Do not wait until you find yourself suddenly approaching the end of your life to laugh, live, and love. Do it now. Do it today. Go to dinner with friends, or make new ones, and laugh. Bungee jump, or learn to surf, or get a tattoo, or do whatever it is that you have not done that will remind you to live. But most of all, love. Love deeply. Take the chance to live your life with open arms and give away as much love as you can. Love is the one thing that comes flooding back to you the more you give.

Gracious God, forgive me for being so busy with life that I forget to live. Help me to receive the gift of dying slowly that I might spend my days laughing, living, and loving. In the name of the One who gave me the gift of life, and life eternal, Jesus, I pray. Amen

Chapter 16 Revisiting Hope

"Learn from yesterday, live for today, hope for tomorrow.
The important thing is not to stop questioning."
Albert Einstein, scientist & thinker

And hope does not put us to shame, because God's love has been poured out into
our hearts through the Holy Spirit, who has been given to us. Romans 5:5

On Sunday afternoon we headed to the beach for a week of "recovery leave." Danelle and I, Jacob, Lydia and Kasey, Lydia's best friend, packed the cars, turned up the music, and headed east to Rodanthe, North Carolina on the Outer Banks. It was a glorious late summer day filled with sunshine, which made the drive enjoyable. We knew this meant we would have to get up very early on Monday because we had the follow-up visit with the oncologists to receive the results from all the scans and tests. That night we sat on the beach until it got dark before heading in for an early bedtime.

Early Monday morning we arose to see the sunrise over the ocean. The salty morning haze made the emergence of the sun difficult to discern, but walking on the beach in the early morning, coffee in hand and the breeze coming in from the sea is still rejuvenating for body and soul. I love the infinitude of the ocean.

The idea of the depths of mystery it holds never ceases to amaze me.

Danelle, on the other hand, is not an outdoor person. If you have never seen a grown woman scream at the sight of dime-sized sand crabs, it is great early-morning entertainment. You see, Danelle does not go outside except to go from the house to the car, and from the car to whatever building she is driving to. While going to the beach was the ultimate vacation for me, Danelle would have been happy to stay inside at home, read mind-numbing fiction, and eat popcorn. So, early on Monday morning she bravely ventured out to watch the sunrise with me and had no idea that there would be "nature" out on the beach. I am sure that the other folks staying in the homes along the shoreline thought there was a mass murderer on the loose from the screaming going on.

By 7:00 a.m. we were making our way north on NC Highway 12 headed toward U.S. Highway 64 West and Durham for my follow-up visit with Dr. Hope. The five-hour drive consisted of random feel-good country songs or a selection of show tunes, depending on who was driving. It is a very interesting emotional and psychological struggle when you know you are going to hear your prognosis. So rather than worry about it, we sang, joked, and pretended I would live forever.

When we arrived we parked in the parking garage and made our way to check in, and made our way back to an exam room to wait tensely for the doctor. We did all the preliminary rituals, verified my birthday, went over my symptoms again, and spoke to another nurse to re-check all of my medical history.

Our new nurse, Sean, was hilarious. Sometimes in the middle of all of the stress of dealing with a difficult situation, you forget to not let it become your whole life. Sean did a great job that day reminding us to keep focusing on living. He gave me his card and said I could call for anything, even if I just needed the joke of the day. He told a joke or two that were so bad I am glad he is a nurse and not a stand-up comedian or his family would starve.

At the appointed hour, Dr. Hope came into the room as her normal, focused, professional self. In some ways she seems like the professional that would be rather unapproachable at a dinner party. In actuality she is quite cordial.

To recap, up to this point all we had to go on was that we had "many months." That vague assessment of my longevity had grown more irritating with each passing day. Having been a social worker, I understand the necessity of ambiguity when describing a patient's situation. It is really all about litigation avoidance, but that does not make it any easier on the patient or his family. When you are sitting in that chair you want answers, even if they are answers you do not want to hear. You want some degree of certainty in an uncertain situation.

We had come with a list of questions. Some of them were serious, like how long could I continue working? Others were, well, not as serious, like whether or not I could get a tattoo. My daughter, Lydia, is trying to convince me that we should get matching tattoos. I wanted to make sure that there was no reason not to get a tattoo and to make sure wherever I got the tattoo would not interfere with future shots or treatment options. Funny, after having a needle biopsy and facing big, honking therapy shots every month, I am still more afraid of some dude with a needle filled with ink who makes his living drawing permanent pictures on people's skin.

I also wanted to know if I could travel. I was offered the chance to go to England in the spring and wanted to make sure I could go. Another question that haunted me was how would the disease progress? What would the eventual symptoms be?

"Pain," she said. "Considering where your tumors are, you may be spared the severe intestinal symptoms, but I would say that you are going to have to deal with some pretty severe pain, maybe worse than you had initially."

Doesn't that sound like fun? That reaffirmed one of my

greatest concerns, that there will be a time when I have so much pain that I will be unable to think clearly. I had spent a day like that in Erie, and it was not pleasant. I wanted the truth, and Dr. Hope is a truth-teller.

Finally, we got back around to how much time she thought I had left. "It's still too early to tell," she said. "We just do not have enough time points to figure out the progression." We did not get certainty, but we did get something. When we tried to get greater clarity, the good doctor finally relented and said that I should be able to work for "a couple of more years." Well, that is clearer than "many months"; but not that much clearer. That did mean I did not have to run home and complete disability paperwork. The research I had been doing about patients with neuroendocrine carcinoid tumors metastasized to the liver gave me an outside chance of making it five more years. One report indicated that up to 30% of patients make it to the five-year mark. I, of course, like any cancer patient, was bravely trying to ignore the fact that this also meant that 70% did not.

In actuality, the survival graph is somewhat depressing. It seems you either live one to two years, or you make it for five or more. That's a tough statistic to see.

The rest of the news? Well, it seems that the cancer had not spread any further than already found. While the primary site was suspected to be a small spot on the pancreas (later we would learn it was between the stomach and the small intestines), the largest tumors were the three on my liver, equaling 17.5 centimeters of combined surface area. There was also some possibility of a tumor on my spleen and some very small spots that could be cancerous in my lungs, but they were actually thought to be old spots from former asthma treatments. Thus far, the tumors had not affected liver function, pancreas, kidneys, or spleen. Overall my labs were very good, all within normal range. So, with the exception of terminal cancer, I was in great shape.

"So when does treatment begin?" I asked.

Have you ever asked a question and not really expected the answer you received? This was one of those times. Treatment began immediately. I mean I left her office, went to the lab for blood work, and then up to the fourth floor to wait for my first shot.

On the top floor of the Duke Cancer Center there are treatment rooms with windows that overlook the beautiful campus. There is a patio with tables and plants if you decide to wait outside. I knew it was going to take a while when I signed in and, because I was a work-in appointment, they then gave us a sheet that said "Why do I have to wait so long?" The sheet explained the verification process for all the chemotherapies they administer. The doctor has to prescribe, the pharmacist has to verify, the nurse has to get the medicine, and then get it approved again by the pharmacist. So you wait.

There was a certain sense of relief that settled in. I would probably be able to work for a couple of more years, so the immediacy had backed off a little more. The presence of death was still there and the cancer was still there, but the feeling of desperation had eased just enough to allow me to breathe. As we sat in the waiting room with a taste of renewed hope, the anxiety that had been resting upon my soul seemed to lift, and before long I was asleep.

My poor wife. I fell asleep on her arm, and she was so concerned about waking me that she sat there for an hour or so, arm going numb, and let me rest. I understand that there is photo documentation that my wife sent to my daughter via her cell phone of me fast asleep in the waiting room. If it ever appears on the web, I have several retaliation pictures of her fast asleep in the car on the way back that might accidentally get released.

Finally, I was called back for my shot. Remember when you were a kid and they gave you shots in your bootie? Yep, this was one of those shots. The needle was about eight inches long and as big as a straw (that might be a slight exaggeration, but that's what if felt like). Being an intramuscular shot, it went in deep and hard. Then it was over. We waited three hours for a five-minute procedure, and then we were on our way home.

When we got to the car — by now close to 4:00 p.m. — we realized that we were starved. In true Cauley fashion, the choice for where to eat was obvious: *Red Robin*! I mean, we had received good news, of a sort. I was not dying immediately; oh I was still dying, but at least more slowly. What better way to celebrate than with a cheeseburger and a chocolate shake? Earlier in the day Lydia, Jacob, and Kasey had sent pictures of chocolate shakes they were devouring at a beachfront soda shop. We thought it only fair to retaliate with our own pictures of milkshakes from *Red Robin*. I have to say that it was the best milkshake I have ever had!

Then, back in the car for the five-hour drive back to the Outer Banks. Have you ever noticed that the drive *back* to somewhere always takes longer than the drive *to* somewhere? I know that it was actually the same number of hours back to the beach as it was to get to Durham, but after a long day of anxiety, waiting, and more waiting, the road seemed to get longer and longer. Somewhere close to 11:00 p.m. we finally arrived back at the beach house to share the news. The kids had decided earlier in the day to have us tell them in person in case the news was worse than expected. So we shared the news, explained that I still have a couple more productive years, and then we would have to see after that. Then we collapsed.

***

The day started and ended at one of my favorite places on earth, at the beach. The beach reminds me of the bigness of God, the expanse of the universe, and the smallness of humanity. It reminds me that while my story is big to me, it is just a grain of sand on the beaches of time. It also reminds me that even though mine is just a small story, the God who created this expanse cares enough about my little-grain-of-sand story to be there for me. The One who scattered the stars in the sky is also the one who is with me in the depths of my despair. I do not know what the next couple of years will hold, but I know Who will hold me together.

Gracious God who created the ocean and the sky, thank you that You love me enough to go with me even into the dark places of my life. It is there where Your light shines through. Thank You for restoring hope when I am hopeless, faith when I have been faithless, and love when I feel most unlovable. In the name of the One who gives graciously hope, faith, and love, Jesus, I pray. Amen.

Chapter 17 Living in Ambiguity

"I wanted a perfect ending. Now I've learned, the hard way, that some poems do not rhyme, and some stories do not have a clear beginning, middle, and end. Life is about not knowing, having to change, taking the moment and making the best of it, without knowing what's going to happen next.
Delicious Ambiguity."
Gilda Radner, actor

"That is why I am suffering as I am. Yet this is no cause for shame, because I know whom I have believed, and am convinced that he is able to guard what I have entrusted to him until that day." 2 Timothy 1:12

The morning dawned bright and clear with the sound of crashing ocean waves and the smell of salt in the air on the first day of my "recovery leave." Tomorrow had come and brought with it the realization that I would be living with an entirely new level of ambiguity in my life. A pervasive uncertainty would always be present as I learned to live with a long-term, terminal illness.

You never really know what tomorrow will hold, even if you think you do. There is always a kink in the plan. There is always an unexpected interruption to your life. Think about it, how many times in your life have things gone exactly as you planned? Yeah, me either. Almost never do things follow the course of the best-laid plans. There is always some ambiguity, but you plan anyway.

On this day we slept in a little longer, had breakfast a little later, and I finally headed to the beach. Knowing my treatment would make me more sun-sensitive than usual I packed a large umbrella so that I could sit on the beach and still have shade. That is exactly what I did. I sat on the beach, almost numb to those around me. I watched Jacob play in the surf and even joined him a time or two. I went back to the house, got a sandwich, and then came back and sat some more.

I love the beach but I am not usually "that guy." I am not usually one who can just sit for hours staring at the surf, but on this day when I was learning to live with my ongoing sense of ambiguity about the future. So much of my life up to this point had been determined by what I was *doing*. What job I had. What task I performed. What challenge I was facing. What role I was playing. Suddenly, that all seemed so insignificant. For the first time in recent memory, I was perfectly content to just "be" and not to "do."

To be honest I cannot even recall what I was thinking. I wrote some in my journal, but not very much. Mostly, I just tried to picture what my new life would look like. What would the "new normal" be? Would there ever be a "new normal?" Or would the dynamics keep shifting and the world keep slipping off its axis every time I thought I had found my equilibrium?

I do not like ambiguity. I like certainty. That seems like an odd statement for somebody who has spent his entire life studying theology, sociology, and human behavior. Each of those things has very little within them that is certain. Theology is the study of God, and that is something humanity has been trying to figure out since prehistoric man stepped out of his cave and looked up at the sky. Sociology is the study of cultures and societies, and if history tells us anything it is that groups of people are awfully unpredictable. Human behavior is the least certain thing of all. Just when you think you have somebody "figured out," they do something that throws all your ideas out the window.

Still, I like certainty. I like stability. I like to understand what happens next. The need to have certainty, stability, and to understand what comes next probably comes from my rather unpredictable childhood. Being the child of a single parent in a low-income home, there was always a prevailing sense of uncertainty. You never knew if the power was going to get shut off, or if your dad would show up for a promised visit, or whether you would be able to buy school clothes. In reaction to that sense of uncertainty growing up, I have always sought to control my life. Sometimes it has worked; usually not. But I have always tried.

Now sitting on the beach, I was becoming painfully aware that the ambiguity I had been trying to hold at bay for my forty-eight years had come to rest on my doorstep and would be a part of my life for the rest of my days, and that sucked. The security I had hoped to give as a gift to my wife by investing in retirement, working for a large denomination with a pension plan, and trying to live responsibly had evaporated. I am thankful that a few years back I had determined to get out of as much consumer debt as possible. The credit cards were paid off, the cars would soon be paid for, and all we would have left was our home. But now there would be medical bills. Big ones. The kind they deliver by UPS in a box. There would be prescriptions and specialists and Hospice care. I am a pastor; I know how quickly those things can add up.

Mostly, however, there was ambiguity. There was the not knowing. Yes, I would probably be able to work for a few more years, maybe longer, maybe not. Yes, I had long-term disability, but that would not be equivalent to my regular salary. Plus, I had no idea how long my resources would have to last. Four years? Six? I hate not knowing.

Funny, isn't it? Along with not knowing comes the idea that you do not really want to know. How would it feel if you had a date on your calendar a year from now, or five, or even twenty, when you knew that was your expiration date? At that moment, on the beach, I kind of thought how freeing that would be, freeing to know the exact date of my demise, because then I would know how to plan. It would be in my hands. I would have some modicum of control. There it is: I wanted control.

Of course, you never really have control. You never really know. You do not have an expiration date tattooed on you somewhere that lets you know just when your time is coming. What you do have is two choices. One is that you can live like you have all the time in the world. The other is that you can live like every moment might be your last. In actuality, you end up living somewhere between those two extremes.

If you live like you have all the time in the world, you fail to ever establish priorities. You float passively through life without direction or purpose. Like driftwood in the ocean, you are pushed and blown in random ways, and you never focus long enough to get anything done. Purposelessness and passivity allow you to take on the role of a victim of fate. Living this way leads to existential crisis, depression, and hopelessness.

The other is also exhausting. If you are living like every moment is your last you tend to try to do too much, cram too much in, and you become exhausted by the struggle. If you are not careful you overindulge, become impulsive, and fail to take consequences into account.

***

So you learn to live in the tension. The tension between living like you have all the time in the world, and living as if every moment is your last. In that tension, if it is managed well, you learn to make the most of every day. You learn to love deeply. You begin to live passionately. You strive to listen to God for direction about every decision. You live in the ambiguity in a way that is healthy and not destructive.

So I sat on the beach and tried to figure out how to live with this renewed sense of ambiguity. I decided to live every day as if I always had tomorrow, but also as if it might well be my last. To love deeply those who God placed in my life. To live passionately each day and try to make the world a better place for my having been alive that day. To listen to God intentionally, and then to do whatever I believed God was leading me to do on that day and in that moment. Then, I could live in the ambiguity.

Loving God who holds all of my tomorrows, help me to love deeply, live passionately, and listen for Your voice and not to the noise of this world. Then help me to do whatever You ask of me on this day, for today is the only gift You have given me. In the name of the giver of life and the keeper of eternity, Jesus, I pray. Amen.

Chapter 18 Why Bad Things Happen to Good People

"If suffering went out of life, courage, tenderness, pity, faith, patience and love in its divinity would go out of life too."
Father Andrew, theologian

Those who live according to the flesh have their minds set on what the flesh desires; but those who live in accordance with the Spirit have their minds set on what the Spirit desires. Romans 8:5

Am I mad at God? Since my diagnosis with neuroendocrine tumors, I have been asked the same questions over and over again. Has my faith eroded with my terminal diagnosis? Do I blame God for getting cancer? Am I angry with God?

I am not angry with God; at least not yet. Oh, I get angry, really angry. I get angry at the situation and circumstance. I get angry at sin, death, and decay. I get angry at the DC. It helps that I had previously defined my understanding and theology of sin. A good theology of sin does not make the sickness any easier, but it allows me to understand its presence in the world, and more personally, in my body. It allows my soul and my mind to grasp, on some level, that I am not being punished. That I suffer, like the rest of the world, from the unintended consequences of humanity's desire to be "like God," instead of desiring to be godly.

Sin entered the world with the act of humanity reaching to be "like God." In Genesis 3:5, humanity performed a deliberate and intentional act of disobedience. It should not surprise us that the prototypical man and woman were disobedient. We are disobedient. I mean, come on, our lives certainly affirm Paul's admonition in Romans 3:23 that *all have sinned and fallen short of the glory of God.*

We wanted our eyes open. We thought we wanted to know good from evil. Unfortunately, the ability to know the difference between good and evil does not give you the ability to control good and evil. It does not even mean you will do good if evil is an option. It just means you will know. And we know. We know and we choose, and often we choose poorly.

I love it when people say "so-and-so fell into sin." That is not what I have seen in my life or the lives of those I have encountered. We do not "fall" as much as we "jump" into sin. We, too, like Eve and Adam, evaluate our options, contemplate the advantages, and bite the fruit. Oh, it is good going down. So good that we make sure we share it with those closest to us. "Here, have some, it is amazing." Then, later, maybe only moments later, regret, guilt, pain, hurt, and fear take up residence in our heart and we know we are busted. We realize that we, too, are "naked," which really means vulnerable to harm and death. It is like those nightmares where you find yourself standing in front of the class with your pants down, embarrassed and ashamed. We blame Adam and Eve, but in reality they are us. If I am honest—if you are honest—we know that we would have eaten the fruit too, and we probably would not have even needed a serpent to point out its benefits.

What we did not know was when we chose to be "like God," that also meant that we opened the door for death to enter. God warned us. God told us that if we chose our way, it would end in death. That we would "surely die." Now we do. We die. Everybody you know has a clock that is ticking. Some of us know ours is ticking faster, but yours is ticking too. I know it, and if you are honest with yourself, you know it too. And despite what we think, we do not really know how much time is left on that clock. Sure, I have become more keenly aware of mine, but in actuality yours could have far less time on it. Every time you cross the street, or walk down the stairs, or live your daily life you could encounter something that would fast forward your life-clock and your alarm could go off. Suddenly, you would be *"absent from the body and present with the Lord."* (Colossians 2:5)

So death is an ever-present reality. In my ministry, I have officiated at more than three hundred funerals and attended many more. I have actually lost count. During the past twenty-three years death has become a frequent companion as I have been with families through long illnesses and sudden, tragic losses. I have stood beside the bed when mechanical means of life support were switched off and watched a senior saint drift into the hands of the Savior. I have cried with grieving parents at the loss of a small child. There is one thing certain about life: it will end. Nobody gets out alive. Sin opened the door, death barged in and has been with us ever since.

So what does this have to do with why I am not angry with God? Because I have always known I was going to die, I just did not know when or how. "The wages of sin is death." (Romans 6:23) The Scripture is pretty clear about that. There is sin in the world and sin in my life. What does sin get you? Death.

So let us recap before we get to the good news. Sin entered the world because we wanted to be "like God" rather than be godly. Humanity knew that once they disobeyed God they would "surely die," but we chose to disobey anyway. Once we disobeyed we were surprised at our own nakedness, or vulnerability, and we were even more surprised that there were consequences to our actions (this sounds awfully much like a parenting lesson so far).

The greatest consequence of our action was that when we opened the door to sin, death came in and became a part of all of our lives. So you do not really get to choose whether you die; you are going to die. Cheery so far, huh? No wonder so many people are on anti-depressants. We earned it because the sins of the world and the sins of our own choosing have condemned us. But there is good news. The good news is the most important "but" in the Bible. The rest of that verse states, "but the gift of God is eternal life through Jesus Christ our Lord." Wait a minute! We deserve death, but we get life?

So how do we get this life? We confess, believe, and receive. 1 John 1:9 makes it clear, *"But if we confess our sins, he is faithful and just to forgive us our sins and cleanse us from everything we've done wrong."* Forgiveness and redemption are only a prayer away.

During times of difficulty it is so easy to ask, "Why me?" That is because we can always think, in our comparative goodness theology, that there is somebody far worse than me that deserves this more than we do. Yes, I have sinned, but I know people who are way worse sinners that I am. So when trouble, sickness, and pain comes our way, what we are really asking when we say "Why me?" is "Why not them?"

When I got sick, I was in pain. I was in a lot of pain. The kind of pain that makes you not fully aware of everything you are saying. I was in the kind of pain where you do not want anyone or anything to touch you. The kind of pain where it hurts to stand up, sit down, lay down, or walk around. There was no comfort. No escaping the presence of the pain. During that time of pain, all I could think of to say was a breath prayer that has become part of my daily life for the past dozen years. I just kept praying, "Jesus Christ, Son of God, have mercy on me, a sinner." Even in pain I knew that because of the sin that was unleashed upon the world, I was just as likely to be the recipient of the consequences as the next person.

I, too, have been guilty of asking God, "Why me?" on occasion. What I am learning to ask, however, is "Why *not* me?" The torrent of suffering has been unleashed upon the world. The wages of sin—death—has flooded our existence. Why do we think that we should live consequence-exempt lives? In a world where genocide happens, where children are starving, and we flood our bodies with chemicals, why do we think that the sin of the world will never penetrate our lives?

If you take the Bible seriously you see that even the saints of God were affected by the sin of the world. We see Lot losing his home because of the sin of the city. We see Paul being beaten, shipwrecked, and eventually martyred because of the sin of the presiding government and intolerant religious leaders. History even shows us the sins of our fellow Christians have perpetrated some of the greatest atrocities. Horrible things have been done in the name of Jesus. Yet, still, we think that we should be exempt from the wages of sin. We are not.

I am going to die. Dying is part of living. Actually dying makes living all the more precious. No, I am not angry at God because I am dying. I am thankful that, as the funeral liturgy reminds us, "even as we die, yet shall we live." Today I choose to live, even though I am dying.

Gracious God who gave me life, help me cherish life, even as I am dying. You who did not spare Your only begotten Son, but allowed Him to come that I might have life, abundant life in this life, and life eternal, grant that I might live as those who are dying and die as those who will live eternally. Amen.

Chapter 19 Duct Tape and Bailing Wire

"Success is to be measured not so much by the position one has reached in life, as by the obstacles which one has overcome while trying to succeed."
Booker T. Washington, teacher, writer, & scholar

So now this is how I run—not without a clear goal in sight. I fight like a boxer in the ring, not like someone who is shadowboxing. Rather, I am landing punches on my own body and subduing it like a slave. I do this to be sure that I myself won't be disqualified after preaching to others. 1 Corinthians 9:26-27

There are some days when somebody asks me how I am doing and I just reply, "I am holding it together with duct tape and bailing wire." It is my shorthand way of saying that there is good news and bad news. The good news is that I am holding it together. The bad news is that at any moment it could explode. I had these types of days before I was sick. Days when I felt that everything could fall apart at any moment, but I always had the confidence that I would have the energy and creativity to put it all back together. That is just it, I was self-confident instead of God-confident. I was self-reliant instead of God-reliant. If DC is teaching me anything it is that, as the children's Sunday School song goes, "I am weak but He is strong." I sang those words as a child so many times, but now I try to live them every day. What does it mean? It means I am learning new lessons about living and dying every day. Here is what I learned those first few weeks. I learned to focus on what I can do, and not be frustrated at my limitations. I learned that it is okay to let other people cry for you and with you. I learned to give God praise in the middle of the storm.

A few years back one of my favorite leadership gurus, Andy Stanley, was speaking at the Catalyst Conference and he said, "Only do what only you can do." I thought, "Yeah right, Mr. Huge Church, Staff-of-Hundreds Pastor, come down to the real world where I preach the sermons, lock the doors, and fix the toilets just to keep the place running" (cynicism is a sin I confess often). That message has come back to me again and again in recent weeks. On those afternoons when I just run out of steam, I have to step back and critically look at all the tasks in front of me and decide which ones I have to do and where can I ask for help. I hate asking for help. I am a "pull yourself up by your own bootstraps" kind of guy.

Growing up in a single parent home, my mother never made more than minimum wage. I worked my way through college, grad school, and post-grad work, usually working full time, and trying to be a fully engaged parent. I have spent years racking up sixty and seventy hour workweeks like badges of honor. I bragged at how seldom I took a real vacation. I was proud of how much I could get done and still have energy to burn. Now at 3:00 p.m. I need a nap, and it frustrates me to no end. I am learning, however, to focus on what I can get done. I am learning, after years of rolling my eyes at the idea, to "only do what only I can do." Yes, things go undone, but it is better to do a few things well, than several things badly. It took DC for me to finally understand that lesson.

I have said over and over again that the only thing worse than being told you have cancer is telling other people you have cancer. This week, somebody who had heard about my diagnosis and wanted to express concern and care stopped me in the grocery story. As a woman who had seen a loved one die of cancer, she was truly empathetic. As tears welled up in her eyes I realized that this happens a lot lately. That just sharing my story, in my sarcastic and somewhat irreverent way, allows people to laugh and to cry for me and with me, and I am slowly getting okay with that. Do not get me wrong, I hate to make people cry, because every time somebody starts to cry, I cry with them. There I am, standing in the frozen food section of Food Lion with tears running down my face and we are talking about how important community is in taking care of those who are left behind.

I think for the first forty-eight years of my life I did not cry enough. I viewed it as a weakness to express my emotions. I am coming to believe that it takes a lot more courage to let the emotions come, wash over you for a few moments, fully live in them, and let them pass, than to stuff them down and keep them pressed into a closed container in your soul. I have to do it because I do not have any more room in my soul for stored emotions; I have to let them out. My willingness to do this also gives permission to those around me, even those who I did not think really cared, to let their emotions out for a few moments too and that is healthy. I still do not like to make people cry, but I am learning to let them, and to cry with them, because they are not just crying for me, they are crying for the hurt place in their life that they have left unattended as well.

In the middle of all this mess I am learning to trust God even in the middle of the storm. I had somebody ask me why I had not abandoned my faith? Why this disease had not caused me, in the words of Job's wife, to just, "curse God and die?" I thought for a while and told them that nowhere in Scripture are we promised cozy comfort and security; that is a postmodern heresy. Like I explained previously, there is sin in the world, and when humanity decided we would be our own gods, unintended consequences that we have trouble understanding were unleashed. In the middle of all of this — in the center of the storm — is where God is always waiting for us. Over and over in the Scripture we are promised that God will never leave us or abandon us, even though we have left and abandoned Him over and over again.

I do not think I did anything to deserve the DC, I know God did not give me the DC; it is a product of sin in the world. What God did was send a solution to the sin when God became flesh and lived among us, died for us, and kicked the hell out of death by conquering the grave in the person of Jesus Christ. In the middle of my storm, when I have insomnia in the middle of the night, I am learning to just lie in the presence of God and know that I can trust God even in the middle of the storm. Oh, I have my doubts, but thanks be to God that I am surrounded by a community so when my doubts overcome me, they believe for me, until I can believe again.

***

So what if it all falls apart? God is with me and he promised that He will put it all back together, eventually. In the meantime, I am buying extra duct tape and keeping spools of wire handy. Do you have somebody you can cry with? Perhaps it is time to find a community to accompany you on life's journey. You never know what is next.

God who loves me, who will never leave me, and who is with me in the middle of the storm, help me to lean on You most when I feel You least. Help me to do what only I can do, love others enough to let them cry and to cry with them, and to dance in the rain in the middle of the storm. In the name of the One far greater than duct tape and bailing wire, Jesus, I pray. Amen.

Chapter 20 Dying To Go On Vacation

"Believe that life is worth living, and your belief will help create the fact."
William James, psychologist & philosopher

Whatever you do, do it for the heart of the Lord and not for people.
Colossians 3:23

Sitting on the beach almost three weeks post-cancer diagnosis, I am wondering why I did not do this more often. Not why I did not sit on the beach, but why did not I go on vacation more often. My typical excuses were:

1. Work—I considered myself indispensable.
2. Scheduling—It seems Danelle and I often have conflicting schedules.
3. Money—I never really understood the value of vacation.

It is ironic that I received my diagnosis on our first twelve-day vacation in seven years. Even that vacation was more serendipitous than well planned. Its agenda was guided by others, but it was a vacation none the less. The vacation was to involve two days of personal time, four days of family time, and then four days in New York City. While in New York, Danelle would be in workshops and seeing Broadway shows, and I was going to play tourist and visit museums, the Statue of Liberty, and consume as much calorie rich food as possible. Like I wrote earlier, my stay in the hospital and our speedy return to North Carolina preempted most of that agenda.

A life coach once told me to put my hand into a bucket of water and then remove it quickly, that would show me how long I would be missed when I left my current job. Yes, for a fleeting instance there would be a hole, but it would quickly heal over. Yes, the volume and mass would decrease, but at the end of the day nature abhors a vacuum and fills one in as quickly as possible.

Most of us work in places and organizations that existed long before we arrived and will be there after we are gone. Even if your organization or company was to shut down, eventually something else would come along and fill the void. This revelation should be both humbling and freeing: humbling because you realize you are replaceable and freeing because you realize the world does not depend upon you.

If we are honest with ourselves most of us are in jobs that somebody else could do better. We just happen to be the current placeholder. I have failed to schedule real time away because part of me thought that the organization I serve would fall apart without my constant attention. I subconsciously believed in a very mechanistic view of the organization that required I constantly keep adjusting the dials to keep it working.

During the past four weeks a surprising thing happened, or did not happen as it were. The organization did not fall apart in my absence. Things kept happening. Worship still occurred. Life went on. I removed my hand from the bucket, and the water filled in the gap.

I do believe I was missed, but I also realize that I am not indispensable. It was truly humbling to realize that if I had to leave tomorrow, somebody would show up to preach next Sunday. Within a month, another pastor would be appointed, and things would continue as if I had never been there. There would still be typical church conflict and the recognition of "God-moments" in the life of the people. All that would change would be the leader, but the church will continue.

This revelation is also very freeing. I now realize how much unrealistic pressure I had been placing on myself. I had acted as though the success or failure of the organization was completely on my shoulders. Funny thing is that people will let you do this because it absolves them of responsibility. If you are able to take all the blame, the other members of your organization can abdicate any personal culpability for its ineffectiveness or floundering.

Suddenly, I am free of accepting the blame for everyone else's unhappiness. I am free to do what I believe God is calling me to do without feeling that the world will end and the church will collapse if I make one bad decision or one big mistake. It also frees me of being subject to the veiled threats of the members and the petty bickering that comes any time you deal with people. Once you are facing the end of your life square on, threats and innuendos based upon personal preferences seem so insignificant.

What really matters is how I am preparing people to face their own eternity and to live passionately right now. Is what I am doing helping them to move ever closer to Jesus? Is it helping them to live in harmony with community? Are they more willing to embrace those searching for God? If not, why should I bother with it at all? I am not indispensable, but I do have important things to get done, including going on vacation.

What is really important? Not being able to make time for vacation has been our most frequent excuse. We just do not have enough time. A pastor's schedule revolves around significant weekend commitments and the needs of others. Think about it, most people take off on weekends, which is when I work the hardest. They take vacation when the kids are out of school at Christmas or around Spring Break at Easter, two of the busiest times on the church calendar. Add to that Danelle's school schedule and our non-profit's summer camp schedule, and finding time to escape becomes a scheduling nightmare.

We have tried to be intentional about some time to ourselves. We hold as sacred our annual spiritual retreat. This time of worship, learning, and spiritual renewal is good for our souls. We also block off Thanksgiving weekend as couple time. We send our kids off to visit their other parents and grandparents and spend the time in an intentional "stay-cation." This time usually involves blockbuster movies, lots of reading, resting, and serious "couple time."

All other time, it seems, usually fell victim to the tyranny of the urgent. When we planned something, a crisis arose, a need came up, or an issue surfaced that needed immediate attention. Our planned time away evaporated. Before we knew it, our calendars were packed and there was just no time left for vacation. We were so busy "doing" that we forgot to practice "being," including just being together. We had plenty of time, it just did not seem that important at the time…how wrong we were.

I really cannot tell you how many times I have said, "I will rest when I am old." Now there is a pretty good chance I will never get "old." The mortality index for my condition is fairly intimidating. I always assumed I would have a decade or two of retirement. The actuarial tables were tilted in my favor. My dad lived to be seventy-two despite smoking heavily and drinking continuously the last four decades of his life. My mother is in her mid-80's and has smoked since before I was born. As for me, I exercise three times or more per week, have never smoked, and I watch what I eat. In actuality, except for the cancer, I am in the best shape I have been since I was twenty-five. I do not participate in high-risk activities, I do not own a motorcycle; and I have a job that, while stressful, is not usually fatal. The odds said I'd live to be 104…now I will be delighted to reach fifty-two. I looked up and what I thought was middle age has become "late in life."

Now I wish I had taken more vacations. I wish I had spent more time just being with the people I love most. I wish I had shared more experiences. But I always considered vacation and time away as an unnecessary extravagance rather than a soul enriching necessity.

***

Do not wait until you are dying to go on vacation. I know it is a pain to pack everything up to be gone for a week. I know it is a hassle to negotiate the time off. I know it is a struggle to work the expense into your already-strained budget, but a week of experiences, board games, and rest with your family is more important that a new car or expanded cable. It does not have to be expensive but it does have to be intentional. Time away does not just happen. It is not an accident that you go on vacation. So save your quarters and go before you wake up one day and realize it is too late. Do not wait until you are dying to go on vacation.

Gracious God forgive me for postponing joy. You have given all of creation and declared it "good." Forgive me for being so busy building my own kingdom that I forgot to celebrate the beauty of what You have created and enjoy the relationships you have placed in my life. Thank You for the gift of life, and help me, oh God, to love deeply, live passionately, and listen to You intentionally. In the name of the One who promised abundant life, Jesus, I pray. Amen.

Chapter 21 Life Lessons from Living While Dying
Love Deeply, Live Passionately, & Listen to God

"I expect to pass through life but once.
If therefore, there be any kindness I can show
Or any good thing I can do to any fellow being,
let me do it now, for I shall not pass this way again."
William Penn, Quaker & statesman

We do not preach about ourselves. Instead, we preach about Jesus Christ as Lord, and we describe ourselves as your slaves for Jesus' sake. God said that light should shine out of the darkness. He is the same one who shone in our hearts to give us the light of the knowledge of God's glory in the face of Jesus Christ.

But we have this treasure in clay pots so that the awesome power belongs to God and doesn't come from us. We are experiencing all kinds of trouble, but we are not crushed. We are confused, but we are not depressed. We are harassed, but we are not abandoned. We are knocked down, but we are not knocked out.

We always carry Jesus' death around in our bodies so that Jesus' life can also be seen in our bodies. We who are alive are always being handed over to death for Jesus' sake so that Jesus' life can also be seen in our bodies that are dying. So death is at work in us, but life is at work in you.

We have the same faithful spirit as what is written in scripture: I had faith, and so I spoke. We also have faith, and so we also speak. We do this because we know that the one who raised the Lord Jesus will also raise us with Jesus, and he will bring us into his presence along with you. All these things are for your benefit. As grace increases to benefit more and more people, it will cause gratitude to increase, which results in God's glory.

So we are not depressed. But even if our bodies are breaking down on the outside, the person that we are on the inside is being renewed every day. Our temporary minor problems are producing an eternal stockpile of glory for us that is beyond all comparison. <u>We do not focus on the things that can be seen but on the things that can't be seen.</u> The things that can be seen do not last, but the things that can't be seen are eternal.

2 Corinthians 4:5-18, underlining added

So what have I learned? What has this struggle with ambiguity and uncertainty taught me? What conclusions has looking squarely into the eyes of my mortality helped me to grasp? I have learned that life is a precious gift, never to be taken for granted. I will celebrate the gift by eating more cheeseburgers, Dairy Queen Blizzards, and enjoying those experiences with those I love. I will have to do what I should have been doing all along, and that is managing my life more intentionally. I have limited reservoirs of energy and I have to make sure I do what is most important each day. I have learned about the importance of vacations. I will be looking for chances to go places on my "bucket list."

All of these lessons have made me truly thankful for the life I have been given and the life I have left. Knowing that I am dying has allowed me to develop a "life theme." It has caused me to create a set of lenses through which to view my life and determine my priorities. I am going to choose to love deeply, live passionately, and listen to God intentionally. I think I have spent my life thus far trying to do these things, sometimes better than others. Now that the clock is ticking even louder, I want to make sure I give them even greater attention. Let me share them with you the way I shared them with my congregation.

Is the love of Christ shining in your life? When you realize that you are deeply loved by God, it enables you to love deeply.

Often we do not really love deeply; we love cheaply. In our social media saturated world where with one click you can delete, unfriend, and remove social contact with another person faster than you can get served at most drive-thru restaurants, we have forgotten the importance of real intimacy. Real intimacy is hard work. Loving deeply is a decision, and it is tough. Loving deeply means you make the decision to love unconditionally, express it wantonly, and nurture it deliberately.

Love with conditions is not love; it is a contract. It is a mutually beneficial exchange of services by people who have similar interests and who affirm one another. To love deeply is to practice 1 Corinthians 13 as a way of life. The famous "love chapter" of the Bible is read at almost every wedding. The funny thing is that the writer of this chapter never married. He did not intend it to be a wedding planner's fall back text. He intended it to be a way of life. If you really read the list, it is intimidating:

"Love is patient, love is kind. It does not envy, it does not boast, it is not proud. It does not dishonor others, it is not self-seeking, it is not easily angered, it keeps no record of wrongs. Love does not delight in evil but rejoices with the truth. It always protects, always trusts, always hopes, always perseveres. Love never fails." 1 Corinthians 13:4-8a

I can hear you now, "Are you kidding me? That is impossible. Have you met my mother-in-law?" Or co-worker, or that guy at church (yes, people at church are sometimes the hardest to love), or whomever else God has placed in your path. Here is one of those hard truths that I have realized as I look squarely at the end of my life: there is nobody for whom Christ did not die. Whether I like them (or love them) or not, God loves them.

If you live life according to 1 Corinthians 13, you are going to get hurt. There are people you can love who will never love you back. Love them anyway. There are people that will use your vulnerability against you. Love them anyway. There are people who will unfriend you over a simple misunderstanding, delete you when you do not affirm their political view, despise you when you are trying to do your best. Love them anyway.

Just like mine, your clock is ticking. Do you really have time *NOT* to love deeply? No, you do not. Do not waste the precious gift of your life on grudges, petty differences, or even big offenses.

The other thing I have learned is that unforgiveness mostly hurts the unforgiver. When you choose to nurture lingering disdain rather than love deeply, you are really hurting your own heart. You are poisoning your own soul. Most of the time those who we unfriend do not know and do not care.

How many times have you been in an argument and brought up all the stuff from the past as extra ammunition? Love is unconditional or it is not love at all. Paul tells us in 2 Cor. 4 that *"the same one who shone in our hearts to give us the light..."* What light are you shining? Are you reflecting the unconditional love that God gives you in Christ? Are you showing it?

To love deeply also has to be expressed wantonly (I love that word, it means excessive and unrestrained). It means living with an open heart, open homes, and open hands. Like loving without condition, expressing it wantonly means letting others know they are loved with your words and your deeds.

Do you tell the people in your life that you love them? Having been with dozens of people as they were dying, I cannot tell you how many times people have said, "I wish I had told my son (or daughter, or friend, or wife) how much I loved them." We presume too much; we affirm too little. A moment of awkward discomfort can heal a decade of pain.

Do not just say it, show it. Expressing love wantonly is more about actions than words. Words can quickly become cheap if they are not affirmed with action. Your mother was right when she said that people judge what you do far more than what you say.

So love is unconditional. It should be expressed wantonly,

but it also must be nurtured deliberately. Love is not accidental. It is a decision. It is a daily decision. It is a risky decision. Love is more than an emotion. Love is also an act of the will. If left unattended, love can quickly turn into resentment. Love, nurtured over time, creates intimacy and vulnerability.

"We are experiencing all kinds of trouble, but we are not crushed. We are confused, but we are not depressed. We are harassed, but we are not abandoned. We are knocked down, but we are not knocked out." 2 Corinthians 4:19

Living passionately is the opposite of living passively. When I was in high school, two things happened almost simultaneously and changed the way I looked at my future: I read Stephen Covey's *Seven Habits of Highly Effective People* and I took a Dale Carnegie Leadership course through Junior Achievement. Both of these experiences hammered into my head the importance of resilience, getting back up when you get knocked down. I learned the power of perseverance. There were three lessons that stuck out to me then and I have since re-visited them, they help me focus upon living passionately and keeping my focus on what is significant: be proactive, begin with the end in mind, and accept the worst but work for the best.

Living passionately means we must be proactive, not reactive. We let life happen to us rather than being proactive. When I have lived as a reaction to my circumstances I have regretted it. There are times when life stinks. Bad things happen to good people. Long before Vince Lombardi said, "It's not how many times you get knocked down, it's how many times you get back up," Paul wrote, *"We are harassed, but we are not abandoned. We are knocked down, but we are not knocked out."* So get up. Make a plan. Get moving. When you get the news my family received on July 10, 2013 you have two choices: get busy living or get busy dying. It is your choice.

Living passionately also means beginning with the end in mind. I have often made the joke that I wanted a thousand people at my funeral. What I meant is that I wanted to look back at my life and know that I had helped people get connected to God, to others, and to their divine calling. I have always had "an end in mind" but now it is even more pressing. Now that I have limited energy, I have to begin every day thinking "what is the most important thing I can do for God today?" If you are busy loving deeply and you have a picture of what you want your end to look like, focus is clearer.

Living passionately also means I accept the worst and work for the best. Death is inevitable. I have an 8:10 chance of dying in the next five years. Here is something to think about, if you are over 40 you have a 2:10 chance of dying in the next five years; and that chance increases by 20% every decade after that. Nobody gets out of this life alive. What are you putting off?

I have accepted the worst, but I am working for the best. I love deeply and live passionately. I am trying to do everything I can to leverage the situation. I am all in for the cause of Christ. What are you putting off? Where are you being reactive?

"Our temporary minor problems are producing an eternal stockpile of glory for us that is beyond all comparison. We do not focus on the things that can be seen but on the things that can't be seen. The things that can be seen do not last, but the things that can't be seen are eternal." 2 Corinthians 4:18

Our world is loud, and God usually whispers. Culture defines success by what you gather; significance is defined by what you give.

I have been reading *Daring Greatly* by Brene' Brown. One thing she said really stuck with me. She contends that most of us define our lives by what we lack. Our self-definition revolves around the statement, "I am not _____ enough." (I am not smart enough, rich enough, pretty enough, small enough, big enough, fast enough, etc.)

I grew up never thinking I was enough. My father abandoned me; I was not a good enough son. I was cut from almost every sports team I tried out for: I was not a good enough athlete. I did not get to go on our honors class trip to Washington because we did not have the money, I was not wealthy enough. I was never the best at anything. I was never enough because in my mind if you were not the best, you were not enough. Every time I have had any set back, it reinforced my not being enough. I have spent my whole life trying to prove myself. Facing my mortality has caused me to understand that I am enough because Jesus says so.

We focus on scarcity when we serve a God of abundance. God made you. Jesus redeemed you. The Spirit inspires you because you are worth it. You are enough. You are the *YOU* God created you to be. The key is to quit giving credence to the voices in your head that tell you that you are not enough and listen to God, who declares you worthy. Listen for God to whisper to you when you study the Scripture; when you worship, and when you spend time loving deeply and living passionately. God will not make you listen. God invites you to listen. The question is: are you listening?

Loving God, help me love deeply; live passionately; and listen to You intentionally. Let me not settle for cheap imitations of love, passive lives, or ignoring Your voice. Thank You that Jesus has made me whole and holy, and that because of Your love, I am enough. In the name of the One who came to love me that I might truly live, Jesus, we pray. Amen.

Last Words

"Finally, brothers and sisters, whatever is true, whatever is noble, whatever is right, whatever is pure, whatever is lovely, whatever is admirable—if anything is excellent or praiseworthy—think about such things. Whatever you have learned or received or heard from me, or seen in me—put it into practice. And the God of peace will be with you." Philippians 4:8-9

May you have food and raiment,
A soft pillow for your head.
May you be half an hour in heaven
Before the devil knows you're dead
Celtic Blessing

This bonus chapter is from my wife, Danelle, especially for those who love and care for us along the journey.

Bonus Chapter for Caregivers: Bags of Bricks

A roller coaster began this journey and a roller coaster will serve as the ending...for now. As the spouse of someone who is chronically and terminally ill with a slow growing cancer, there is a roller coaster that is part of my regular routine. As my husband, Marty, has ups and downs with his well-being on this journey, so do I. My roller coaster travels alongside of his, but mine goes up when his goes down. Anyone who has shared the journey with a loved one will recognize this ride.

As Marty begins to take a downward turn on his journey, I begin to gear up. I get ready to battle with him and for him as his strength wanes. My body goes into fight mode with much adrenaline that gives me the "super powers" I need to get him through his crisis.

As Marty stabilizes, my body begins to shut down. The adrenaline subsides, the "super powers" go dormant, and the energy needed for the crisis drains away. And I feel horrible physically, mentally, and emotionally. As Marty's roller coaster climbs higher to take him back to his normal level of energy and well-being (or the "new normal" dictated by cancer), my coaster dips alarmingly quickly and I hit rock bottom.

This cycle became crystal clear to me when a couple who are very dear to us were diagnosed with cancer just over a year after our diagnosis. In this case the wife is suffering from melanoma which apparently can metastasize to the breast tissue and other places without you ever finding a tell-tale spot on the skin. I dropped by to visit my friend, Virginia, as she was recovering from a downward turn and responding well to her current treatment program. She was enjoying the fact that she was beginning to feel like she had enough energy to live her life again. I took the family one of Marty's famous lasagnas to use on a day when they needed some help and our chat grew into a nice, long conversation.

After about 30 minutes her husband, Garry, came in and sat down with us. He looked like hell. I told him so. He described how he had been anchoring Virginia though her crisis the previous week and that now he was wiped out completely. It clicked for me in that moment that this was the exact cycle I had repeated multiple times during the last year. I told them that was exactly what happened to me each time Marty went into a crisis. Garry seemed relieved that someone else could relate to the journey they were on.

So...being the spouse of the cancer patient pretty much sucks out loud. It changes everything and it changes nothing. I still am madly in love with my husband and count him as one of the greatest blessings that God has ever trusted me with. We are still that couple that makes people gag a little bit because we are completely connected and have a wonderful relationship. That has not changed. The fact that we have an "ending" written into our story a little bit earlier than we imagined has changed. It makes the sweet moments sweeter and the tough moments tougher.

Back during the initial period where we were telling everyone about our diagnosis, I had another friend share her very personal response with me. This was a friend that I encouraged Marty to call personally after the initial immediate calls to family, work, and closest circle. He agreed that we needed to tell Loretta fairly quickly because as a massage therapist she tends to know all of the gossip in town before it actually happens. When he called I was nearby and could tell that she was not saying much at all.

The next time I saw her she almost fell to pieces. She explained that during the call she had fallen to her knees and alarmed her fiancé who was sitting in the same room. When she got off the phone she shared the news with her daughter who, after having a near death car accident in her younger days, has a healthy faith life and is fairly tuned in with God's plan for the world. Loretta was lamenting that it was not fair that we had this to face since we were obviously meant for each other, had both come out of difficult first marriages, and had been married for only 7 years. Loretta was telling her daughter that it was not fair for me (Danelle) to have finally found my knight in shining armor only to lose him so quickly. Her daughter's response to the question of why God would allow this, still gives me goose bumps.

She told her mother that while it was true that Marty was my knight in shining armor, maybe God put us together for Marty's story and not mine. Her idea is that maybe God allowed Marty to have the wife who would see him through this horrible experience to the end with love. Maybe God did not want Marty (who is actually an extreme introvert at times) to have to face this alone. Wow. Yeah…still chokes me up!

Cancer does not fix things. If you have a crappy relationship going into the diagnosis it does not magically make you the perfect couple. If you have a great relationship with the normal ups and downs associated with being human, it doesn't magically ruin your relationship. You are on the journey together and the patterns you have established are the patterns that emerge as you continue forward. Marty and I can laugh together, cry together, love together, be still together, and pray together. Cancer is simply now part of our journey.

Being the spouse, the caretaker, the cheerleader, the publicist, the shoulder, the warrior, the advocate, the phone receptionist (aka interceptor)…is daunting. And it is worth it. You need a break sometimes. You need one more than you will be willing to take one. If you do not take a break you will break down. So…Marty and I are very productive people. We go, and go, and go. People joke about Energizer bunnies around me regularly. Yet,I still need more breaks and permission to give myself more grace because I am carrying this load, too. I am not the one stuck with the treatments (literally for Marty since it is an intramuscular shot) or the pain. I am the one "stuck" with watching my life partner suffer through it all never knowing when the next crisis will hit.

Virginia and Garry's daughter is the same age as my son. I see her at our school and have worked with her in theatre productions (did Marty tell you I am a theatre teacher?). One day at the end of school I was passing Cameron in the hall and she looked as tired as I felt. We had both already laughed together about how people don't know what to say to us and how they give us a special look and tone of voice to ask how we are doing. In case you did not know, you are apparently supposed to tilt your head slightly, take all signs of joy from your face, and lower your pitch and volume to ask, "How are you?" to anyone who has a very sick family member. As I looked at Cameron this day, I could see her heavy journey. I asked her if she was tired from carrying her bag of bricks around. She got it immediately. The weight of having a loved one with cancer feels like living life while carrying around a bag of bricks with you. It is always there. In the background. Clinging to you. Cameron got the metaphor and pantomimed picking up a backpack of bricks and pretended to see my bag on my shoulder, too. Yeah…it's yucky sometimes and laughing at it with someone who gets it helps a bunch!

This chapter is supposed to encourage the loved ones. I do not know how to do that exactly. Assume that your response is normal even if you are crying your eyes out one minute and making cancer jokes the next. Assume that your response is normal if you want to pull your loved one closer than ever and also need some space to yourself. Assume your response is normal if you forget things and cannot quite do everything as exactly as you did before. It is tough to keep up when those bricks want to drag you down!

Be kind to yourself. Drink more water (yes, I tell everyone this all the time). Sleep more. Rest more. Laugh more. Cry more. Let go of things more. Ask for help more—and be specific. Forgive the people who do not help after offering over and over again to do so. Thank the people who do help. Forgive yourself for not somehow transforming into a real superhero who can handle the crisis perfectly at all times (including the bricks!) Forgive your partner for getting sick. Forgive yourself for needing to. Embrace joy and don't worry about pretending to be happy in front of others. You can do it. God put you on this journey and He is with you every step of the way. (And yeah…forgive Him for that, too!)

Resources to Help You Cope

Centering Prayer resources for learning the basics of this powerful meditation process and how it can help you manage the stress of a chronic or terminal illness. (centeringprayer.com)

Mindfulness resources Not into prayer? Click this link for the basics of mindfulness practices to help you cope with illness, stress and life difficulty. (mindful.org)

Sun Realty Time to head to the beach? Give my friends at Sun Realty a call to get a great deal on a beach vacation! (sunrealtync.com)

Alpha Tours Betty Ann Buckley is one of the best travel agents around. Give her a call at Alpha Tours to check a few things off your bucket list! (alphatours.com)

My Invisible Life is an excellent blog for those of us suffering from mostly invisible illnesses. It is a great place to find inspiration to keep going on dark days! (myinvisiblelife.net)

Dr. Marty Cauley's personal blog is a combination of personal coaching, cancer stories, and his work giving direction to new faith communities. (www.MartyCauley.org)

Neuroendocrine Cancer Support

The Healing Net Foundation was founded by individuals with a common desire to bring neuroendocrine cancer from the obscurity of the "cancer that Steve Jobs had" to a level of understanding that neuroendocrine tumors are very treatable forms of cancer; many patients can live long lives of high quality. We understand it first-hand, as patients or friends of patients. This is an excellent site for the latest information about treatment options and updates on research.

Carcinoid Cancer Foundation Basic information about neuroendocrine carcinoid cancer including an excellent introduction to the disease, treatment options, and even a list of specialists by state. This is a great place to start if you were recently diagnosed.

NET Patient Foundation This is another great resource for support, information, updates on clinical trials, and keeping up with what is happening in the NET community.

Duke Cancer Center Special thanks to the phenomenal staff of the Duke Cancer Center who have helped me with my journey!

This is a bonus chapter from Dr. Cauley's next book *Welcome to a Life that Matters*. This book will help you discover and live the divine calling that is within you. This one month spiritual journey will guide you through a process and then help you put a plan into action so that you can live a life that matters. Look for it later this year along with a sermon series and daily journal to inspire you to live a life that matters!

Bonus Chapter from
Welcome to a Life that Matters:
The First Choice

Romans 12:1-2

"Therefore, I urge you, brothers and sisters, in view of God's mercy, to offer your bodies as a living sacrifice, holy and pleasing to God—this is your true and proper worship. 2 Do not conform to the pattern of this world, but be transformed by the renewing of your mind. Then you will be able to test and approve what God's will is—his good, pleasing and perfect will."

You have a divine calling. Yes, you. Whenever I tell people that God has a plan, path, and purpose for their lives, they get this blank look in their eyes and shake their heads just like you are doing now. Let me guess, you got this book because you have been struggling with some of the following questions:

Why am I here?
What difference can one person make?
What is my real purpose in life?
What is next for my life?
How do I know what God wants for me?

Paul writes in Romans to a people similar to you who were trying to figure out this whole "God's will" thing. I mean it sounds good when a preacher stands up with a big Bible and tells you to live in the center of God's will, but nobody ever tells you how to figure out what that is in an understandable way. For the next twenty-eight days I want to invite you to spend some time every day learning to hear God's voice and then deciding to do whatever God would have you do. That is a big request, let me say it again, learn to hear God's voice, and then be willing to do whatever God asks you to do. I know a lot of people who never really strive to listen to God because they are afraid that God will ask something big of them. Guess what? He will! That's what God does. God asks us to give up the easy for the sake of the eternal. Welcome to a life that matters!

There are many forces in your day-to-day world trying to impose their ideas upon what your calling should be. Depending upon how much media you consume you are subjected to between 3,000-10,000 advertising messages per day. Per day! That's more than your grandparents probably received in an entire year. Every one of those messages is trying to convey to you that you will be happy, fulfilled, or content by adding whatever product or service they are selling. If that's not enough we are subjected to pop psychologists yelling at us from radio or television to modify our behavior or asking "how is that working out for you?" Well, it's not. Chances are you are a little less content and a little more anxious this year than you were last year. You have the feeling that you are missing out on something, that maybe God has a divine calling for you that you haven't discovered. For the next twenty-eight days I want to take you on a journey to help you discover what your divine calling is.

Go back to the beginning of this section and read that short piece of scripture again; I'll wait. Paul wrote this letter to the church in Rome because they kept getting the inside and the outside mixed up. People thought that faith was about how they acted on the outside—the kind of friends they had, the kind of clothes they wore. People were trying to impress each other. Sound familiar? They kept confusing "schema" or being conformed to this world with "*metamorphia*" or being transformed from the inside out. When you accept Christ as your Lord and Savior, you are transformed by having Christ formed within you. That radical reworking reshapes who you are from the inside out.

I believe one of the biggest obstacles to Christ-followers being who God designed them to be is their unwillingness to answer their divine calling. Every day of your life has led you to this moment. God can take every trial, every experience, and all of your stuff and carve out of it a way for you to make an eternal difference in this world and in this community. You have to be willing to seize your calling. Once you seize your calling you will be leading a life that matters!

Prayer for the journey: *God, you have called me to die to sin and break the mold of this world. You sent Your Son, Jesus, to come into this world so He could enter my life and begin making me new from the inside, not from the outside like the world. I invite you IN to begin making me new and ask you to help me be willing to hear your voice and be willing to do whatever you are calling me to do. In the name of Jesus, the Savior and the giver of second chances I pray. Amen.*

I am working on a sequel to *Dying to Go on Vacation* that deals with living with a long-term, chronic, terminal illness. I plan to include guest chapters from others facing a similar journey. If you would like to share part of your story contact me at marty@martycauley.org. Your story could help others cope on *The Long Road Home.*

Bonus Chapter from
The Long Road Home
Battle on Three Fronts
Lord, you brought me up from the grave, brought me back to life from among those going down to the pit. Psalm 30:3

I have not been well. Since the middle of December, with the exception of a few days around Christmas, I have been struggling with my illness. I am nineteen months into the battle for my life and the past month has been the most difficult time of struggle thus far. I have had every symptom imaginable it seems. I've had night sweats, fevers, nausea, headaches, joint pain, tumor pain so bad I had to go to the hospital, dehydration, and the list goes on. I have had entire days where it was exhausting just to get out of bed and try to keep food down. What nobody warned me about was that one of the issues with having a long-term, terminal illness is that it is a battle on three fronts. It is a fight for body, mind, and soul. Your body is not your own. Your mind begins believing the worst. Your soul seems to shrivel against the weight of the attack.

When you deal with a long-term illness it seems like your own body has betrayed you. The ironic thing about my illness is that prior to falling ill I was in the best shape of my adult life. I was eating right, exercising faithfully, and striving to manage stress. I was sleeping well and I had more energy and felt more in control than I had in decades. I was determined to enter my fifties fit and strong. Then my body betrayed me. Some cells went rogue, cancer started to grow, and by the time it was detected I had multiple lesions in multiple places and my best hope is to slow the growth of the tumors and treat the symptoms. On January 1, 2015 I had my second, serious carcinoid attack. My tumors woke me up from a dead sleep with pain like I had not felt since my initial diagnosis. I literally could not stand up straight. If that wasn't bad enough, I was 500 miles from home and I knew the community hospital close by would not know what to do. After some serious pain medication and IV fluids they discharged me. For the next two weeks my body heaved and wretched and seized in ways I never imagined. I felt like I was becoming a mere shadow of myself. That is when the body began to affect the battle of the mind.

During dark days of physical struggle even the most positive of us (and I am NOT the most positive of us) can begin to believe the worst. I remember sitting in my chair shaking from chills while my face flushed hot from the hormones being released by my tumors thinking, "What if it never gets better than this? I don't know if I'm strong enough to handle this kind of pain indefinitely." Your thoughts tend toward catastrophizing the situation. The pain and fight within your body causes you to begin to think very small. You can only focus on whether you can eat something and actually keep it down. Or whether you can drink enough not to become dehydrated again. Taking a shower seems like an aerobic workout. You feel small, useless and helpless. Then around the edges guilt creeps in. You feel guilty for all the things you have to ask others to do for you. You feel guilty for missing work and knowing you are letting people down who expect you to perform. You feel guilty that you can't power through this and force yourself to do more. You try to stay positive, but the pain impacts the brain. Before long the battle on the third front is also raging, the battle in your soul.

People tell me I'm strong. I am not. I am stubborn, but I am not strong. During some of those darkest days it felt as if my soul shriveled within me. One night as I lay in bed with Danelle I told her that I was pretty sure I was strong enough to handle a fast, terminal disease, but I'm not sure I have the strength to endure this marathon to the end of my life. This slow plodding march to decline seemed too much to bear. It is hard, and it is hard every day. I've never been a big fan of the Psalms. Sometimes they seem a little whiney, but during the past month I understand the depths of sorrow at feeling abandoned by God. I know that God did not abandon me, don't flood me with Christian hyperbole and "footprints" poems, but when you are in the "depths of despair" you feel abandoned. Your body is in pain, your mind is thinking the worst (and the worst is not death, it is thinking that the struggle will never end), and your soul can hardly continue to believe. You are down to your last shred of faith. The tattered remnants of hope that you cling to in the dark of night are all that you have left. Now the battle on three fronts is raging within you.

In the midst of the battle on three fronts what got me through was remembering. Remembering that God was with me, had suffered for me, and had experienced real suffering upon God's own self in the person of Jesus upon the cross. Remembering that the community of faith that I am part of was believing for me. When it seemed my soul had shriveled to nothing, I remembered that others were praying and believing for me, standing in the gap between my doubt and God's presence. Remembering that I do not have to be strong. In the midst of my doubt, pain, guilt, and struggle it was okay that my strength was not enough. Death has already been conquered, it is not up to me to win, my task is to remain faithful with whatever I have left.

The battle on three fronts is not over. The struggle will continue. There will be other difficult, dark days. Thank God for those of you who will continue to hold the candle for me when my hand shakes and my strength fails. Thank God for those of you who will believe for me when doubt overwhelms my soul. I, like the writer of Hebrews, can say that I am surrounded by a "great cloud of witnesses." I am not strong, but you are strong for me, so I continue to fight on three fronts.

Acknowledgements

Thanks to my many friends who have read, edited, and critiqued the many forms of this book. Thanks to my first "proofreader" and editor, Danelle, who also happens to be my wife. I'm glad you were almost an English major! Thanks Lisa Creech Bledsoe, writer, editor, and boxing champion, the first professional editor and friend who kept pushing me to keep writing and to finish. I am blessed to call you friend. Thanks Tammy Benfield who read and reread to help catch my myriad of grammar and typing errors. To Suzanne Rollman who saved me from the pain of cover creation, edited photos, and understands living with ambiguity like no one else I know. To Bishop Hope Morgan Ward and Reverend Jeff Severt who created a position flexible enough for me to continue in ministry while I battle cancer. To my older brother and sister, Donna and David, who have always believed I could do anything I set my mind to and who didn't laugh at me when I was a child and told them I wanted to be a writer. To my mom, because I am her favorite. To my blog readers, Facebook friends, Twitter followers, church members, and online friends, your comments have been most gracious and your support invaluable. To my team at Duke Cancer Center (Hope, Margo, Tracy, and the amazing nurses, aides, and staff), you are the best team a cancer patient could have. Lastly, to cancer fighting ninjas and carcinoid zebras, I am praying for you! May you find the strength to love deeply, live passionately, and listen to God! I am humbled to be walking this journey with you. This book is for you!

About the Author

At twelve years old Marty told his family he wanted to be a writer. Now, thirty-eight years later he is finally living the dream while facing death.

Coming from a low-income home in Raleigh, North Carolina he learned the value of hard work, determination, and getting back up when life knocks you down. From his first job mopping the floor at the local Piggly Wiggly to serving as a pastor in a struggling community he has always thrown himself into everything he has done. His passion for life and desire to invest in others have made him stand out in the communities he has served.

Fueled by a love for gourmet coffee, Eastern North Carolina BBQ, and a desire to make the world a better place, Dr. Marty Cauley currently serves the North Carolina Conference of The United Methodist Church as Director of Content and Coaching. He is a professional ministry and life coach committed to helping individuals, organizations, and congregations stay focused on what really matters most.

An ordained elder in The United Methodist Church, he previously spent five years traveling the Southeast as the Director of Ministry with Young People for the Southeastern Jurisdiction. He has also journeyed to Africa to work with orphans after raising tens of thousands of dollars to fund an empowerment project with ZOE Ministry. He has volunteered in his local community to build homes with Habitat, strengthened his local community by working with a local low-income school, and served as a board member for Peacemakers Family Center. A blogger, speaker, and motivator, he uses humor and story telling to engage his audience and help them find hope during difficult times.

Now Marty is facing the biggest challenge of his life—how to love deeply, live passionately, and listen to God while facing a recent diagnosis of terminal cancer. *Dying to Go on Vacation* is a humorous and sometimes heart-breaking story of dealing with why bad things happen to good people.

Dr. Cauley holds the Doctor of Ministry, concentration in Church and Culture, from Columbia Theological Seminary; the Masters of Divinity from the Divinity School at Duke University; and the Bachelor of Science in Social Work from East Carolina University.

Would like for him to speak at your next event? To schedule him email MarblesPress@gmail.com

Are you looking for some life coaching so you can make the most of your "marbles?" Marty can be contacted at marty@martycauley.org Also follow him on Facebook as MartyJCauley, on Twitter @MartyCauley, and through his blog at www.martycauley.org for updates, speaking engagements, and encouragement. A monthly newsletter is coming soon! Sign up for it on his blog.

Responses to *Dying to Go on Vacation*

"Marty Cauley writes with truth that flows from his heart...something this journey has changed. Although I have always aspired to be as smart as my dear friend...now I hope to be as wise. Learn from his wisdom...it will change your heart." Dr. Laura Early
Founding Pastor and Community Developer
All God's Children United Methodist Church

"Marty Cauley speaks candidly of intrusive illness and the unwelcome journey he and his family now make with cancer as a part of every day. We see in his life the undeniable interweaving of abundant and eternal life in the life he now lives to God before us all. Read this book and give thanks for the life, abundant and eternal, we share in Christ." Hope Morgan Ward
United Methodist Bishop, North Carolina Conference

"I continue to be inspired by Marty's ability to speak his truth simply, slowly, and beautifully. Thank you Marty for not shrinking from death, but meeting it head-on, with God's love and trust for life now and life to come. One of the best reflections and narratives about life and death I've read in a long time." Rev. P. Drake, Chaplain

"I love your description of dying slowly. You put into words of wisdom to love, live, and laugh." Donna P., Cancer Survivor

"The Psalmist urges us to "teach us to number our days, that we may gain a heart of wisdom". In Dying to Go On Vacation, we discover a heart of wisdom in the transparent witness of Marty Cauley. As I read his testimony, I connected his story with crises I have navigated in my own life, and I thought of brothers and sisters who are passing through present storms. I am happy to commend these lessons, which have a life and death urgency, to a wide audience!" Bishop Kenneth Carter
United Methodist Bishop, Florida Conference